The Model Prayer

Twelve Studies on How to Pray

J. Gordon Henry, Ed.D.

Other books by J.Gordon Henry
A Christian's Necessary Food
Adoration: Prayer as Worship
The Enabler
Intercession: Prayer as Work
Notes from My Bible
Prayer Seminar Workbook
Spiritual Warfare

Dedication

To the *Board of Directors* whom God
has given J. Gordon Henry Ministries as
faithful counselors and supporters:

Susanne Adams (Mrs. Robert)—Since 1987
Sue Webb Bell (Mrs. Tommy)—Since 1984
Don Edwards—Since 1988
Sue T. Henry (Mrs. J. Gordon)—Since 1984
Juanita Hutchins—Since 1992
Paul E. Jennings—Since 1984
Archie King—Since 1996
F. Murray Mathis—Since 1984
Loretta Mathis (Mrs. F. Murray)—Since 1988
Rebekah Summar (Mrs.Robert)—Since 1996
Patricia Vaden (Mrs. Patrick)—Since 1996

Honorary:
Barbara Custalow (Mrs. Lin)—Since 1984
Lin G. Custalow—Since 1984
Katherine Goff Morgan (Mrs. Frank)—Since 1984
Glenda Holland (Mrs. John)—Since 1985
John Holland—Since 1985

Preface

Prayer is the key that unlocks all the storehouses of God's infinite grace and power. The Lord Jesus Christ has given us a pattern for powerful praying in the Model Prayer.

Power in prayer is available for anyone, anytime, anywhere, who agrees with the pattern and follows the principles laid out in all circumstances.

There are nine movements for effective praying which we will study in detail to the end that our praying will reflect the pattern given by Jesus in His Sermon on the Mount in His answer to the one disciple's request: *"Lord, teach us to pray."* (**Luke 11:1**). You already know the prayer; now note the movements:

1. *"Our Father which art in Heaven"*
2. *"Hallowed be Thy name"*
3. *"Thy Kingdom come"*
4. *"Thy will be done on earth as it is in Heaven"*
5. *"Give us this day our daily bread"*
6. *"Forgive us our debts as we forgive others"*
7. *"Lead us not into temptation"*
8. *"Deliver us from evil"*
9. *"For thine is the kingdom, and the power, and the glory forever"*

Both Martin Luther (1483-1546) and John Wesley (1703-1791) stressed the importance of following the pattern. Luther said, "The Lord's Prayer is the highest, noblest, and best prayer; all other prayers shall be suspected which do not have or contain the content and meaning of this prayer."

A disciple is a learner. If followed in a spirit of spiritual exploration, these very practical studies will lead believers into exceedingly rich and powerful communication with the Heavenly Father in a "Sweet Hour of Prayer." The Model Prayer is an appropriate place to begin for those who want to learn to pray. The prayer is so comprehensive that Archbishop William Temple said: "It is the prayer you will offer if you love God with your whole heart."

As this book goes out, my sincere prayer is that the readers will be blessed and strengthened by reading and studying this material as I was in preparing it. The preparation has made a tremendous difference in my own understanding of prayer. I believe the same will be true of those who are ready to move upward and onward to newer vistas in their own daily time with God.

This book is meant as practical help for people who want to grow in prayer. Study may be on an individual basis or in a group.

Yours in Calvary love,

J. Gordon Henry
Murfreesboro, Tennessee

b

Study One

And it came to pass, as He was praying in a certain place, when He ceased, one of His disciples said to Him, *"Lord, teach us to pray, as John also taught His disciples."*

Luke 11:1

The Lord Jesus Christ, during His earthly sojourn, gave prayer top priority in His life and ministry. This becomes obvious as you read the account of His life provided by Matthew, Mark, Luke, and John in their Gospels. To prioritize is to order according to importance—a concept we are familiar with as we prepare daily or weekly "to do" lists. If there are ten things to do, the most important thing to do is ranked first and the least important last. For Jesus, prayer was high on His list.

Example
Twenty-one vignettes are given of Jesus praying. Thus, His example supports the importance of prayer in His life and work. Prayer was the work He did before doing other work. It was not preparation for the battle, it was the battle itself. In addition, He teaches about prayer twenty-one times—"how to" pray and "how not" to pray. The total references to prayer in the life of Jesus total forty-two—a fact that is dramatic, indeed, within itself. It is helpful to be alert to see prayer in His life as you read and study the Scriptures.

Expectation
How many times does Jesus need to express His will in any matter for it to be implemented in our lives? One time would surely suffice. But in three consecutive expressions which are recorded in **Matthew 6:5, 6:6, and 6:7**, He repeated *"When* [not **if**] *you pray, pray like this."* This affirms that He expects His children to pray.

Explanation
A remarkable truth is that the Lord accented the importance of prayer not only by His example and His expectation, but by His explanation. He explained "how to" pray and "how not" to pray.

Any teacher or preacher would do well to understand clearly the significance of this approach to maximize learning. Nothing is easier than using opportunities to share the Word as times to tell people **what** to do—which is needed, but falls short of helping them get a handle on the truths to bring into their daily living. When this is the approach, it is easy to send sincere Christians off on a guilt trip. Good teaching is not only saying what to do, but providing help in how to implement the truths.

In my own ministry, my style from the beginning was to preach the Word, but to use my time to tell people **what** to do— never mentioning **how** to do it. I wanted my sermons to be sensible, spiritual, and scriptural. Basically, my style of preaching for a quarter of a century was topical preaching— which means that I took a topic and built a message around it supporting each idea with scriptural truths quoting the verses and citing the references. No one could allege that my messages during this long period of ministry were not scriptural. The missing element was providing suggestions that moved beyond **what** to do to **how** to do it. Once I understood the pattern of Jesus was to share **how** to do it, as well as **what** to do, I consciously changed my long-followed approach. The response of my people was very positive and appreciative. This principle is carried over to the prayer seminar ministry in which I am engaged as the basic approach to all that is shared.

"How to" Scriptures

It is amazing that 10% of the Sermon on the Mount (**Matthew 5,6,7**)—one out of ten verses—deals with prayer. The basic approach taken by Jesus was to deal with both "**how to**" and "**how not to**" pray statements. Although one would do well to study the Sermon on the Mount (**Matthew 5:6,7**) to understand basic prayer truths taught by the Lord Jesus Christ which are critically important, the basic theme of this study and studies which follow is the Model Prayer—which is a part of the Sermon on the Mount.

Objectives of studies

The work which must come before all other work for the Lord is prayer work as is evidenced in the "Greater Works" passage (**John 14:12-14**) which has as its context asking in Jesus' name. Believers need to be taught to pray for themselves. You and I do not have to walk alone and we do not have to be defeated. Further, the need is to mobilize believers who are on praying ground to become intercessors. An intercessor is one who stands between God and other people or circumstances. The work of the Lord needs prayer warriors. The people of the world need prayer warriors. As the population of the world approaches six billion, it is sad to report as many as two of three have never heard the name "Jesus" in a saving sense one time. This is not because God has favorites, but there are no intercessors praying for laborers as Jesus Himself instructed God's children to do (**Matthew 10:34-35, Luke 10:2, John 4:35**). To encourage believers to become prayer warriors is the basic thrust of the twelve studies in this book.

The Model Prayer

"The Lord's Prayer" is a term which is common to everyone—even many who never attend church services. It is to be noted, however, that the term is misdirected. Following the Upper Room Discourse found in **John 13, 14, 15, and 16**, the true Lord's Prayer is contained in **John 17**. In fact, the entire chapter is His prayer.

In response to one disciple's request (**Luke 11:1**), Jesus shared a prayer to serve as a model for our praying. Because prayer was central to His life and ministry, He wanted the disciples to understand its role in theirs as well. Rather than being "The Lord's Prayer," this prayer could well be identified as the Model Prayer. It is important to remember the Model Prayer was not given as a prayer to pray—rather, it is a prayer to teach us how to pray. Actually, He says, "*in this manner, therefore, pray*" (**Matthew 6:9**). Then He provides the model to follow—listen and pray like this.

Profound, eternal concepts are compressed into sixty-six words—a few concise phrases shining with enduring brilliance. When fully grasped by us, they can overturn much of our wrong thinking about God and about prayer. In a sense, the Model Prayer is a teaching device based on an outline to be taken over and filled in with our own words expressing our needs.

It is possible to pray this prayer as your prayer if doing so is not simply automatic and ritualistic. In fact, if your heart is not in it, saying the words could be regarded as using His name in vain! There is abundant evidence that God would not only reject such action, but would "hate" it! The same is true in reading Scripture or singing a hymn with His name in it—and our heart is not in it.

During this initial study, a wide scope lens will be used to view the Model Prayer as a whole and determine the skeleton of the prayer. In future studies, a zoom lens approach will be used to enable examination of each plank in the treatise. Phrase by phrase, the Model Prayer can be applied to every person's situation and need. It is timely and timeless. Each of us can make it ours so that its phrases will carry the burdens and joys of our hearts to the Heavenly Father.

Prayer addressed to the Father

Jesus pointed out that prayer is to be addressed to the Father. Prayer is always **to** the Father, **through** the Son, **in the power of** the Holy Spirit.

In essence, Jesus amplified this truth when He pointed out to the disciples in the Upper Room Discourse that once He returned to the Father they could do something that they had never done before. They could go directly to the Father in His name—**to** the Father, **through** the Son. During the days following His death, burial, resurrection, and ascension, I am sure that they spent time in meditation and reflection on the meaning of prayer. It is still true that the only access to the Father is through Jesus (**John 14:6**). It is through His merit and His authority that we can approach the Father.

For one reason or another, many believers address their prayers to either the Lord Jesus Christ or the Holy Spirit. Certainly, one can talk to Jesus and the Holy Spirit during times of prayer. Jesus, however, gave as the model addressing prayer **to** the Father.

Two Overall Directions

This Model Prayer will order our prayer lives if we will follow it. Note that the Model Prayer can easily be divided into two sections using the pronouns which are prominent. Note that prayer begins with God, not us. The first half is the pronoun "Thy"—Hallowed be "Thy" name, "Thy" kingdom come, "Thy" will be done. Of course, this means that prayer is above all else to be God-directed, not man-directed. Reverence is prayer's first requirement. Humility is a requisite of prayer because only out of that comes the praise of God's greatness which gets prayer started.

Although there are times when a person might not begin His prayer with worship—as did Peter when He was about to drown! (**Matthew 14:30**), a basic pattern of praying should be to begin with worship and praise—indicating a deep, abiding interest in the things in which the Father Himself is interested. In fact, I have found many times that after a time of worship, many of the items on my prayer list did not appear as pressing or demanding as they had when I approached the Throne of Grace. Do you know what I mean?

4

The second half of the prayer features the pronouns "us" and "our." Give "us" this day "our" daily bread. Forgive "us" "our" trespasses. Lead "us" not into temptation, but deliver "us" from the evil one. There is no doubt that a believer must learn to pray for himself and others. What is it that I need to help me "be" what God wants me to "be" and "do" what He wants me to "do"? Pray about it. The problem arises when we approach the Throne with "us" and "our" items which are so pressing and neglect to acknowledge in worship and dependence the One who can do something about the needs we have.

Prayer is not only to begin with praise, it is to conclude with praise.

Conclusion

Some maintain that the Model Prayer is not for believers today and disparage any effort to put it into our lives as Christians. I don't believe that at all. As we study together, let's determine what lessons we can learn from the teaching of our Lord Jesus Christ as He responded to the obvious need to provide a model or pattern for praying.

Praying the way God wants us to pray is a worthy goal for each of us. You will find the pattern is just as relevant and timely today as it was two thousand years ago when Jesus gave it to His disciples in ancient Palestine. The challenge which the Model Prayer gives us is to bring our minds and the feelings of our hearts into harmony with its implications as the most effective way to strengthen our prayer lives.

It is important to remember, however, that the only way to learn to pray is to pray. It will make a difference when you and I actually pray following the pattern. Try it and you will be awed at the beauty of the pattern.

Begin by praying, "Our Father in Heaven." Center your mind on what it means to talk to the Creator of the universe as Father. Pray to the Father about the Father—His person, "hallowed by Thy name," His program, "Thy kingdom come," and His purpose, "Thy will be done on earth as it is in Heaven."

Then pray about His family—for provision, "Give us our daily bread," for pardon, "forgive us our sins, for we also forgive those who have sinned against us," and for protection, "Lead ... deliver us from the evil one."

The amazing thing you will discover is the purifying effect on the content of your praying. You won't be able to pray for things that exalt your name, advance your kingdom, or promote your will. You won't be able to ask God for daily bread if you

5

have a spirit of independence relying on your own strength. You won't be able to ask God to forgive you when you are unwilling to forgive someone else. And you won't be able to ask for His protection from the evil one when you are playing with sin in your own life.

May these studies on the Model Prayer reassure our hearts, strengthen our resolve, and lead us into personal contact with God, our Father, on a higher, more meaningful level than ever before. May its beauty and serenity draw you to a deeper walk than ever before. May you become a prayer warrior.

Study Two

"And when you pray, pray like this ... "

Matthew 6:9

Many Christians are confused about prayer. Others feel frustrated and are often defeated in their daily prayer lives. While most people pray, relatively few people pray to God on His terms. Praying the way God wants us to pray is something we are addressing in these twelve studies. The Model Prayer was given to resolve all the confusion and to bring to believers the fullness of prayer from the perspective of our Lord Himself. Prayer itself requires a strong measure of discipline; so does learning about prayer.

The Model Prayer, one of the most familiar of all prayers, is much repeated, but little understood. The instructions from Jesus are as relevant today as they were 2000 years ago. How we are to pray is specifically and comprehensively covered in sixty-six words in **Matthew 6:9-13**—a section of the Sermon on the Mount. At another time and place, Jesus taught the prayer in response to the request of one disciple which is recorded in **Luke 11:1-4**. Both contain the same skeleton or framework. Although the basis of our studies will be the account in the Sermon on the Mount, it will be well to review the account in Luke.

The disciple's request

For two years, Jesus had worked with the men He had called "to be with Him" (**Mark 3:24**)—His disciples. They knew not only His teachings, but His life since they had front row seats to observe His every move. They had witnessed His miracles. Yet, as far as we know, they never came to Him and said, "Lord, teach us to preach," or "Lord, show us how to minister." One disciple, on behalf of all them, did come and request, "Lord, teach us to pray."

We usually ask an expert to give us the best he has to offer. When we're with a successful financial advisor, we ask, "Teach us to invest." From a gifted scholar, we request, "Teach us how to study and do research." Jesus' disciples asked Him, "Teach us to pray." They knew He was an authority on prayer as they observed the way Jesus made prayer top priority in His life.

Because prayer was central in His life and ministry, Jesus wanted it to be vital in the lives of His disciples, so He responded

7

by giving them what is commonly called "The Lord's Prayer." Actually, the prayer is misnamed because the Lord Himself could not have prayed, "Forgive us our sins."

Some maintain that the prayer should be more appropriately labeled "The Disciple's Prayer" because it is aimed for His followers—a primer on prayer for people like us. My own preference is to call it "The Model Prayer." The prayer is not so much a prayer to be prayed as it is a prayer to teach us how to pray—to serve as a model for our own prayers.

The response: a blueprint, pattern, outline, model

A blueprint is useful for a builder when he constructs a building. A pattern directs each step of the tailor in making a suit. An outline assists a speaker as he prepares a speech. The Model Prayer is a blueprint, a pattern, and an outline providing the Lord's perspective on prayer for us to learn and follow. No believer needs to be without insight on prayer; there is no need for him to proceed in his prayer life on trial and error. In fact, every basic thing one needs to know about prayer is included in this masterful, brief teaching on prayer. We have the blueprint, the pattern, and the outline to guide us.

We can be confident that the Lord Jesus Christ, the Master Teacher, covered the points His disciples needed to follow to learn how to pray.

A familiar passage of scripture is the Sermon on the Mount (**Matthew 5,6,7**) in which Jesus gave the characteristics of kingdom citizens in contrast with the religious leaders in His day. He expected a different level of living from His followers reminding them that their righteousness must exceed that of the Scribes and Pharisees. The context of the Model Prayer is the Sermon of the Mount.

To understand the importance of prayer in the mind of the Lord Jesus Christ, note that 10% of the Sermon on the Mount deals with prayer—one of ten verses. Basically, Jesus deals with both "how to" pray and "how not" to pray.

It is interesting to observe that in the Sermon on the Mount, Jesus dealt with three public forms of worship: almsgiving, praying, and fasting. He basically pointed out that motive was central in acceptable worship. Many of those listening had the wrong motive—a desire for the notice and commendation of men which resulted in hypocrisy. The scribes and Pharisees who practiced prayer so openly, prominently, and frequently did not really want to be holy before God, but only wanted to appear holy before men. They wanted the reputation of righteousness as they gave, prayed, and fasted, but they did not want the reality of righteousness. Their walk did not match their talk.

A major point to focus on is that a good act can become a cause for God's condemnation if it is wrongly motivated. An example outside the Sermon on the Mount is Paul's teaching in **1 Corinthians 13**. All eloquence (including eloquence in prayer), all faith, all knowledge, and even self-sacrifice carried to an extreme of martyrdom, are useless and "*profit nothing*" apart from the motivation of love. When the motive is wrong, our religious activities are but "*wood, hay, stubble*" which will one day be tested by fire (**1 Corinthians 3:12-15**). That which does not pass the test will be burned up and there will be no reward in Heaven.

In two brief, concise and clear declarations, James—through the inspiration of the Holy Spirit—provided remarkably helpful insight into prayer: "*You have not because you ask not . . . You ask and don't receive, because you ask amiss*" (**James 4:2b,3a**). The word "ask" is the word "pray" and is used for prayer wanting God's hand to move—for God to **do** something for yourself or others. Many Christians simply do not pray; others do pray, but have no answers because they ask "amiss." "Amiss" has to do with wrong motive in praying. It is possible to do a good act and still not be approved by God when the motive is wrong. He asks the embarrassing question, "*Why did you do it?*" This is the point Jesus is making in the Sermon on the Mount as He deals with motive in giving, praying, and fasting.

The scribes and Pharisees zealously and assiduously practiced the public forms of worship—giving, praying, and fasting. But their desire for the attention and commendation of men reduced their activities to hypocrisy. A hypocrite is a person who does not want to **be** holy before God, but only to **appear** holy before men. Instead of being concerned about having the **reality** of righteousness, he only wants the **reputation** of righteousness. The sense of "hypocrite" is the Greek actor's wearing a mask to portray someone he is not—which is the origin of the word.

As He spoke of hypocritical giving, praying, and fasting, Jesus used a Greek word that cannot be adequately translated by one English equivalent. It is *apechoo*, made up of the preposition *apo* meaning "*from* " and the verb *echoo*, meaning "*have.*" It is translated "reward" in the King James version. When this term is used, it indicates **BEING PAID IN FULL WITH NO BALANCE LEFT OVER**. When rent was paid, this compound *apechoo* was used. The person received a receipt marked "**PAID IN FULL!**"

Jesus was teaching that when a person gives so he can be commended by onlookers, he is "paid in full" on this earth and God will have nothing for him in Heaven. On the contrary, when a person gives not to receive commendation from men, but to please and glorify God, there will be reward in Heaven. The same is true of those who pray publicly to be seen of men. They have their full reward in this life. **Prayers meant for the ears of men will never reach the ears of God.** The same principle applies to fasting motivated by the wrong purpose.

Prayer was not a new idea for the Jews in Jesus' day. Rather, prayer has been a major part of the lives of many Jews from their early history. Remember **Genesis 4:26b**: "*then began men to call upon the name of the Lord.*"

Building on the Jewish heritage, Jesus provided information about the characteristics of Kingdom citizens in the Sermon on the Mount and established for all time that prayer is vital to their lives—**but it must be properly motivated to be acceptable.** Those Jews who were listening must have been shocked because they gave prayer priority. The only problem was that they had perverted the meaning and activity of prayer until they simply were only communicating with themselves as is illustrated by the man who went to the temple to pray and talked to himself, and not with God (**Luke 18:9-14**). Their motives were quite different from the motives that God honors as revealed in the teaching of the Lord Jesus Christ.

Actually, the Jews should have known and included in their praying the things Jesus taught. Old Testament Jews believed that they had a right to come to God in prayer and that He wanted them to come. Their coming was not like pagans, in fear and trembling. Their rabbis taught, "*The Holy One yearns for the prayers of the righteous.*" The psalmist stated, "*The Lord is nigh unto all them that call on Him*" (**Psalm 145:18**) and "*he shall call upon Me, and I will answer him*" (**Psalm 91:15**).

Further, the rabbis believed prayer was a mighty weapon that released God's power. One of the interesting statements in the *Midrash*, a Jewish commentary on some Old Testament scriptures, says: "*A human king can hearken to two or three people at one time, but he cannot hearken to more. God is not so. For all men must pray to Him and He hearkens to them all simultaneously. Men's ears become satisfied with hearing but God's ears are never satisfied; He is never wearied by men's prayers.*"

10

Jewish teachers taught that prayer was to be constant, not just an act when a person was in trouble. The Jewish **Talmud** directs *"Honor the physician before you have need of him."* Pray before misfortune comes.

The Jews were aware that Old Testament Scriptures directed that certain elements should be incorporated in prayers:

• **A sense of awe and reverence in the presence of God's holiness.** When Isaiah came face to face with God, his response was holy awe: *"I am a man of unclean lips, and I dwell in the midst of a people of unclean lips: for mine eyes have seen the King, the LORD of hosts"* (**Isaiah 6:5**).

• **Confession of sin.** David talked about the need to get sins cleansed before he could experience the presence of God: *"I will wash mine hands in innocency: so will I go about Thine altar, O LORD"* (**Psalm 26:6**) and the only ones who can come into the presence of the Lord are those with *"clean hands, and a pure heart"* (**Psalm 24:3-4**).

• **Loving praise.** The psalmist says, *"I will bless the Lord at all times; His praise shall continually be in my mouth "*(**Psalm 34:2**) and *"O LORD, open Thou my lips; and my mouth shall show forth Thy praise"* (**Psalm 51:15**).

• **Thanksgiving.** Jonah said, *"I will sacrifice unto Thee with the voice of thanksgiving"* (**Jonah 2:9**). The psalmist called out: *"Bless the Lord, O my soul, and forget not all His benefits"* (**Psalm 103:2**).

• **Humility.** A true Jew came to prayer to submit to the will of God. Prayer is bringing self into conformity with God's will, not to ask God to do our will.

• **Perseverance.** Moses spent forty days before God on the Mountain. When God revealed to him that the children of Israel were sinning by worshipping the golden calf and He was ready to consume them, Moses prayed earnestly that God would forgive them and did not give up until God relented (**Exodus 32:11-14**). And that is perseverance.

Consequently, the Jews had a great heritage of genuine prayer, but something went wrong. Jewish prayer became hypocritical. Jesus pointed out that they prayed *"to be seen by*

11

men" (**Matthew 6:5**). Their motive was selfish—trying to gain things for their own ends in a public display.

When there are violations of the truths laid out by Jesus, having full knowledge of the meaning of the Model Prayer will make no difference. In fact, one engaging in the act of praying ignoring His teaching related to correct motive is guilty of hypocrisy—the major problem of the scribes and Pharisees.

Jesus reiterated the ingredients of prayer from Jewish tradition. What He said, therefore, was not totally new. Although what He taught added richness beyond anything known in the Old Testament, everything was in harmony with what any Jew familiar with the Old Testament knew already.

The Model Prayer

The Model Prayer is the skeleton on which you can hang every prayer ever prayed—it is virtually a pattern for all praying as you will see through thorough study. Let's note some of the areas covered.

God-believer relationships

The Model Prayer unfolds the relationships a believer has with God. There is a Father-child relationship, so we say, *"Our Father."* There is a Deity-worshiper relationship; thus, we pray *"Hallowed be Thy name."* *"Thy kingdom come"* is a Sovereign-subject relationship, while *"Thy will be done"* is a Master-servant relationship.

Further, a Benefactor-beneficiary relationship with God is reflected in *"Give us this day our daily bread."* A Savior-sinner relationship is shown with *"Forgive us our trespasses."* *"Lead us not into temptation"* is a Guide-pilgrim relationship.

Direction specified: Godward, then manward

There are seven elements laid out in the Model Prayer. The first three are Godward and can be followed by studying the pronoun **"Thy"**: *Hallowed be **Thy** name, **Thy** kingdom come, **Thy** will be done.* **"Us"** and **"our"** are the pronouns highlighted in the manward section of the prayer which includes four elements: *Give **us** this day **our** daily bread, Forgive **us** our trespasses, Lead **us** not into temptation,* and *Deliver **us** from the evil one.*

Isn't it amazing that much of our praying today violates the set order Jesus taught? It is important to be sure that God has His rightful place—which is first, not last. Placing God in the supreme place makes sense. It is clear that the first three

12

elements show the purpose in prayer: to hallow His name, to bring in His Kingdom, and to do His will.

God's means highlighted
There is **provision** as God gives us our daily bread, **pardon** as He forgives our sins, and **protection** by keeping us safe from the evil one's influence. We can be sure that God is exalted in His glory, in His Kingdom, and in His will as He provides, pardons, and protects.

God's roles manifested
The first purpose of prayer is to hallow the name of God, then to bring in His kingdom, and His will. As a **Father**, He gives us our daily bread. As a **King,** His Kingdom comes when He forgives and pardons our sins to the end that He reigns and rules in our hearts. The will of a **Master** is done as He leads us away from temptation. Father, King, Master are roles which can easily be seen fleshed out in the Model Prayer.

Past, present, future
Asking for sins to be forgiven is for the **past**, asking for "daily bread" is for the **present**, and "*lead us not into temptation*" is for the **future**.

Physical, mental, spiritual
All facets of life are touched in the Model Prayer. Bread is physical; forgiveness to relieve the anguish of guilt is mental; temptation is spiritual.

Alliteration
Beautiful alliteration can be used to outline the Model Prayer:

PATERNITY:	*"Our Father"*
PRIORITY:	*"Hallowed"*
PROGRAM:	*"Thy Kingdom"*
PURPOSE:	*"Thy will"*
PROVISION:	*"Daily bread"*
PARDON:	*"Forgive us"*
PROTECTION:	*"And lead us not and deliver us"*
PREEMINENCE:	*"For Thine is the kingdom, and the power, and the glory forever."*

Reciting the Model Prayer

A Christian has missed the point when he simply recites or says the Model Prayer, although He could pray the prayer if His heart is in it and he makes it his own. But Jesus did not give the prayer to be recited. He gave it to teach His disciples how to pray. How can we be sure this is true?

First, the prayer was taught on two different occasions and is recorded twice (**Matthew 6** and **Luke 11**) with the wording differing somewhat. If Jesus was giving a prayer to be memorized and recited, He would not have used different words the two times He gave it.

Second, the request was, "*Teach us to pray,*" not "*Teach us a prayer.*" It is one thing to recite a prayer; it is another thing to know how to pray.

Third, Jesus clearly warned against using "*vain repetitions*" (**Matthew 6:7**). It would be ridiculous to think that He immediately gave a prayer to be repeated in direct violation of His teaching.

Four, there is no record in the entire New Testament where this prayer was repeated by anyone. It is a model prayer—a prayer to teach us how to pray, in what manner to pray. It is the skeleton upon which we are to flesh out.

The Model Prayer, then, is not so much a prayer to pray as it is a prayer to teach us how to pray. To fail to grasp this truth and respond accurately would certainly be a travesty indeed.

Message never changes

My mother-in-law, the late Willie King Troutman, was a most remarkable lady. Not only did she keep a diary—with daily entries—she kept scrapbooks beginning in her pre-teen years. After the death of her husband, my father-in-law, Rollie A. Troutman—her children meticulously went through the house and disposed of their earthly possessions.

One of Mom Troutman's scrapbooks, probably prepared when she was eleven or twelve, was given to Sue as a keepsake. Two newspaper articles deal with the death of President Warren G. Harding on August 2, 1923, and the swearing in of Calvin Coolidge as the new President in his Plymouth, Vermont home. Although the pages are yellowed, brittle, and frazzled, Sue and I spent considerable time turning the pages and thinking about her life. The scrapbook is full of clippings—articles, poems, sayings, cartoons, beautiful pictures. One saying in her handwriting dated and signed on November 29, 1922, is a wise one which she wrote "KEEP FOREVER. *Count that day lost*

14

whose low descending sun views no worthy action done." Isn't that a worthy guideline?

One scrapbook entry which touched me entitled "The Model Prayer—A Beautiful Version Made in 1823 and Picked Up During the War of the Rebellion" follows:

OUR FATHER
Thou to the Mercy Seat our souls doth gather
To do our duty unto Thee
To whom all praise, all honor should be given
WHO ART IN HEAVEN,
For Thou art the Great God
Thou, by Thy wisdom rul'st the world's wide fame
HALLOWED BE THY NAME.
Forever, therefore,
Let nevermore delays divide us from
Thy glorious grace, but
THY KINGDOM COME,
But let Thy commands opposed be by none,
But Thy good pleasure and
THY WILL BE DONE
And let our promptness to obey be even
The very same
ON EARTH, AS 'TIS IN HEAVEN.
Then, for our souls, O Lord, we *also* pray
Thou would'st be please to
GIVE US THIS DAY
The food of life, wherewith our souls are fed,
Sufficient raiment and
OUR DAILY BREAD,
With every needful thing do Thou relieve us
And of Thy mercy, pity
AND FORGIVE US
All our misdeeds, for Him whom Thou didst plea.
To make an offering for
OUR TRESPASSES,
And for as much, O Lord, as we believe
That Thou wilt pardon us
AS WE FORGIVE
Let that love teach, wherewith Thou dost acquaint us,
To pardon all
THOSE WHO TRESPASS AGAINST US,
And though, sometimes, Thou findst we have forgot
This love for Thee, yet help

15

AND LEAD US NOT
Through soul or body want, to desperation,
Nor let earth's gain drive us
INTO TEMPTATION
Let not the soul of any true believer
Fall in time of trial
BUT DELIVER
Yea, save them from the malice of the devil,
And, both in life and death, keep
US FROM EVIL.
Thus pray we Lord, for that of Thee, from whom this
may be had
FOR THINE IS THE KINGDOM,
This world is of Thy work, its wondrous story
To Thee belongs
THE POWER, AND THE GLORY
And all Thy wond'rous works, have ended never,
But will remain forever and
FOREVER.
Thus, we poor creatures would confess again,
And thus would say eternally
AMEN.

Thus, The Model Prayer ministered to hearts during the
Civil War, as it has to all generations since the Lord Jesus Christ
taught it. To be effective in our prayer lives today, we must pray
in the very manner He has directed when He said "*when you
pray, pray like this!*"

Infinite truths
Someone has said that the Model Prayer has so many facets
that studying it in depth is similar to holding a many-faceted
diamond up before the light. With every turn, there is a new
facet.
Only God Himself could produce such a model; no human is
capable of what He has given to us. The elements, the wonders,
the beauties of the Model Prayer are almost infinite.
As we look at each element in future studies, let us resolve to
come out understanding not just the parts which make up the
whole, but the whole itself. The reason we pray is to seek God's
glory—that is the only correct motive in prayer.
The daughter of an atheist once said to a friend: "*I was
brought up without any religion. I do not believe in God.*" And
then she added a little wistfully, "*But the other day in an old*

16

German book, I came across a German prayer. And if the God of that prayer exists, then I think I might be able to believe in Him."

"*And what is that prayer?*" her friend asked. Then she repeated slowly in German The Model Prayer. The Model Prayer is indeed one of the most wonderful proofs of the existence of God. How could there be a thought of God which is so sublime and so beautiful dealing with man's relationship with Him unless there truly be a God? What a wonderful time of study we will have as we study carefully and systematically that prayer. Are you excited? I am!

The Model Prayer is the single greatest utterance of Jesus when viewed within the circle of His own life and thought. In a very real sense it is a portrait of His mind and person. He both lived it and prayed it. It is alive with His dedication and faith in the Heavenly Father as can be seen as you read; it is warm with love and trust; it is deep in moral earnestness; it is bright with His belief in the coming of the Kingdom. It was His very own prayer before He gave it to His disciples—and to us.

Study Three

So He said to them, *"When you pray say,* "*Our Father in Heaven, Hallowed be Thy name..."*

Luke 11:2

Prayer can be a dry, meaningless ritual which is invariably the result of becoming indifferent to the meaning and purpose of prayer. Then we lose touch with God as far as personal fellowship is concerned. At that time, we must rediscover the original meaning—and start all over afresh and anew. There is no better way to begin than knowing and understanding points the Lord Jesus Christ taught in the Model Prayer.

The Model Prayer

One day Jesus had been praying in a certain place. When He finished, one of the twelve disciples asked Him to teach them to pray (**Luke 11:1**). Jesus, the Master Teacher, knew that this was a teachable moment—the learner was ready—and did what the disciple asked, remarkable teaching indeed.

The result was the Model Prayer (**Luke 11:2-6**), commonly referred to as The Lord's Prayer. This prayer, however, is not so much a prayer to pray as it is a prayer to teach us how to pray. It will be helpful to a believer seeking to enhance his time with God to study the model prayer—which begins and ends in worship and praise—and to emulate the teaching by following the instructions laid out by the Lord Jesus Christ Himself.

A moment of review

As I made my heart preparation to prepare this study—the third one on the Model Prayer—the Holy Spirit impressed upon me to begin with an overview of key ideas and information taught in the introductory lessons.

There are two distinct sections in the Model Prayer which can be discerned by noting the pronouns used — *Thy, us,* and *our.* The pronoun in the first half is "Thy"—"Hallowed be Thy name, Thy kingdom come, Thy will be done on earth as it is in Heaven." The pronouns in the second half are "us" and "our." "Give us this day our daily bread. Forgive us our trespasses. Lead us not into temptation. Deliver us from the evil one." After we worship, we are ready to talk with Him about our needs and the needs of others (which is **petition** **and intercessory**

praying). Most have the order reversed with little or no reference to "Thy" and an overwhelming use of "us" and "our."

While it is very important to deal with the "us" and the "our" aspect of prayer, much prayer is ineffective when "Thy" elements are given less than first place—when worship and praise do not have priority. It is one of those cases when "you should have done those things (prayed for yourself and others), but you should not have left the other (worship and praise) undone" (**Matthew 23:23**).

Daily, not a special occasion

Throne room praying reminds us that prayer is not bringing God down to earth; it is going into His presence—an awesome thought. Even having the privilege to come into the presence of the Father—something which no person could ever do before the Lord Jesus Christ returned to Heaven—is awesome as well. It is not our worthiness that opens the door of access; rather, it is the Lord Jesus Christ and His name.

One of the most basic and important passages of Scripture is **John 14:5-6**. How can we know the way to God? Only through His Son, the Lord Jesus Christ. Jesus is the Way because He is both God and man. By uniting our lives with His, we are united with God. We trust Jesus to take us to the Father where all the benefits of being God's child are ours. As the *way*, Jesus is our path to the Father. As the *truth,* He is the reality of all God's promises. As the *life,* He joins His divine life to ours, both now and eternally. He is the only way to God and He declared *"no man comes to the Father but by Me."*

Praise, in prayer, does not change God. Rather it changes you and me. We are much more likely to trust God once we sincerely praise Him. Matthew Henry, writing in the early 1700's, pointed out that we can never add to GOD'S PERFECTIONS. He is already all that He can be. He will never be any greater or more complete than He already is. He is within Himself worthy of our worship. But how do we do it?

A few years ago, I conducted a prayer seminar at the U. S. Hospital for Federal Prisoners in Springfield, Missouri. During a break, one of the inmates, a young man from one of the Western States, shared how he had received Christ as personal Savior and had an intense desire to walk closely with Him. *"Can you help me in my worship in prayer?"* he said, *"It seems I say the same words over and over until my praise is stale."* Have you ever felt that way? How is this aspect of your praying?

19

Prayer touches three worlds: Heaven, looking toward God, which is worship; Earth, looking toward people and circumstances, which is work; and Hell, looking toward Satan, which is warfare. It is important to understand the difference. How is the worship aspect of your prayer life? When you are touching Heaven, looking toward God in worship, is it a fresh, invigorating time of encounter, or is an "oh hum" and routine event?

During our study of this section of the Model Prayer, it is important to keep in mind that our concern is having a time day by day with the Lord—not what we do on a special occasion and detailing what to do during that time. Therein is an exceedingly great danger—in fact, I believe it is the greatest danger facing a true believer. It is awfully easy to become overly familiar with the Holy. When this happens, hallowing His name becomes an empty ritual and the sense of awe vanishes—and the result is awful, indeed. More than anything else, we must focus on who God is until we come before Him with deep, abiding reverence and awe—which means amazement and wonder. To do less does not hallow His name.

Nothing short of a sense of awe is appropriate when we stand on holy ground before His throne and His majesty. Understanding the holiness of God will bring that sense of awe and respect as nothing else will.

Standing on holy ground

Do you remember when Moses had an encounter with the living and holy God at the burning bush? *"Do not come any closer,"* God said. *"Take off your shoes, for the place you are standing is holy ground"* (**Exodus 3:5**). At God's command, Moses removed his sandals and covered his face. Taking off his shoes was an act of reverence—conveying his own unworthiness before God. God is our Father and Friend, but He is also our Sovereign. We must understand that when we come to Him to hallow His name, we, too, are standing on holy ground. To approach Him casually, frivolously, or flippantly shows a lack of respect and sincerity. Further, to come into the presence of holy God carelessly is the height of presumptuousness. How often we are guilt of this very thing. We must be alert to adjust our attitude so it is suitable for approaching a holy God in a comely and appropriate manner.

God gave His people many rituals and instructions to follow in Leviticus to teach them valuable lessons. But over time, the people became indifferent to the lessons.

20

Overly familiar with the holy

Do you remember the story of Uzzah (**2 Samuel 6:2-8**)? There came a day when the Ark of the Covenant—which had been captured by the Philistines at Shiloh—was being returned to Jerusalem. The ark was a box and was being transported on an oxcart. Uzzah and his brother Ahio were enlisted as drivers. En route to Jerusalem, the oxen stumbled, the cart moved, and it looked like the box was going to fall off. Uzzah reached out to steady the ark and the moment his hand touched the ark, he died! Have you ever studied what exactly was the sin of Uzzah? It must have been pretty serious for God to strike a man dead.

Uzzah, for one thing, was the son of Abinadab, a prominent resident of Kiriath-jearim—a hill town northwest of Jerusalem—who had taken custody of the ark when the Philistines returned it (**1 Samuel 7:1, 2 Samuel 6:3-4, 1 Chronicles 13:7**). The ark had been in his father's house for twenty years. Day in and day out, Uzzah had seen the ark. It was a familiar piece of furniture. He had seen it all these years and the ark had become just a box. He had lost his regards for the sacredness of it as a symbol of God's presence among His people. When he reached over to steady the Ark of the Covenant, his intention was to help. The result was his death.

Matthew Henry said, "Perhaps he effected to show before this great assembly how bold he could make with the ark after being so long acquainted with it."

Uzzah was a Levite, but he wasn't a priest. Only the priests could touch the ark (**Numbers 4:15**)—and that only under certain circumstances. We're Levites and priests. It is a sad day when the ark becomes a box—when you and I become so familiar with Scripture and worship that we lose our reverence. Alexander Maclaren said, "*It was a lost case of awe in the case of Uzzah.*" Nothing is more delicate than the sense of awe. Trifle with it ever so little and it speedily disappears. It's awfully easy to become overly familiar with the holy.

Watch the average Sunday morning congregation. You don't see much awe in the faces of the people. What you see is not awe, it's awful. You and I can take God's name in vain without cursing. We do it when we sing, "My Jesus, I love Thee, I know Thou art mine. For Thee all the follies of sin I resign" when we haven't done it. Or when we repeat "Have Thine own way, Lord, Hold o'er my being absolute sway" and don't mean it.

A tourist in Africa chanced on some boys playing what looked like a game of marbles. He drew nearer and discovered

21

they were playing marbles—with diamonds. Because that was South Africa and in those days diamonds were mined and were plentiful. Playing marbles with diamonds! And we are doing that in our churches today.

I heard of a girl who was touring Europe. In Vienna, Austria, she went to the museum where there is kept on display Beethoven's piano. And she sat down and played some rock and roll on it. The old caretaker endured it. And then after it was over he said, *"Paderewski was through here some years ago."* *"Oh,"* she said, *"And what did he play?"* *"Nothing,"* said the caretaker. *"He said he was not worthy to touch Beethoven's piano."*

It's an awful thing to treat the ark like a box—in cheap familiarity the holy things of God. Watch that. Somebody has said there is no greater hindrance to Christianity than a superficial acquaintance with the language of Christianity from childhood. Although that sounds like a superficial statement, it is correct. It is dangerous.

Alone with God

Seeking solitude was an important priority for Jesus. People were clamoring to hear Jesus preach and teach. They came to have their diseases healed. But Jesus often withdrew to quiet, solitary places to pray. His was a busy schedule, but He made room to be alone with the Father (**Matthew 14:23** NIV). Spending time alone with the Father nutures a vital relationship and equips us to meet life's challenges and struggles. There was a day when Jesus fed 5,000 men. Including women and children, some estimate the number to have been at least 20,000. Certainly there was enough need present to keep Jesus busy for days on end. But He sent them away so that He could go pray—alone with His Father. *"After [Jesus] had dismissed them, He went up on a mountainside to pray. When evening came, He was there alone"* (**Matthew 14:23** NIV). Luke observed, *"But Jesus often withdrew to lonely places and prayed"* (**Luke 5:16** NIV).

In the prayer seminar, an effort is made to confront believers with the need to develop the discipline of spending time alone with God on a daily basis. Strength comes from God, and we get it by spending time with Him. You will never know God if you don't spend time in His presence. A time alone with Him helps us grow spiritually and to become more and more like Him. Many things clamor for our attention. We often run ourselves ragged in attending to them. Like Jesus, however, we must take time to withdraw to a quiet place to pray.

22

As I share, I encourage believers to include worship in their personal, daily devotions and explain how to do it (See *Prayer Seminar Workbook*, pages 7, 30-31, 50-51). A key verse to guide worship states "*But the people who know their God shall be strong and do exploits*" (**Daniel 11:32**). There will never be correct worship until believers anchor their worship in who God is. The only way to know who He is requires a knowledge of His revelation of Himself in the Word of God. In the Old Testament (written in Hebrew), there are a number of Hebrew words which are translated "praise" in the English. The basic meaning of the words includes to magnify, to extol, to exalt, to lift up. The New Testament (written in Greek) adds an additional dimension to the meaning of praise and that is to value. Actually, the word *worship* comes from the Anglo-Saxon word, *worthship*.

Begin with hallowing His name

All prayer comes from need. You and I need to have time in our prayer lives to go before God with no other reason than being with Him—to love and to adore Him. The first purpose of prayer is to know God and to be able to worship Him rightly.

Several years ago, I conducted a prayer seminar for the Mennonites in Pennsylvania. When I said that all prayer comes from need, a lady raised her hand to ask a question. "*Are you sure*," she inquired, "*that all prayer comes from need?*" I answered, "*Tell us what you are thinking.*" She responded, "*I was thinking of the times in prayer when I go to God just to be with Him and not ask Him for anything.*" My reply was, "*I am not going to answer your question, but I want you to think about it for a moment and then you answer your question.*" Very quickly her countenance changed, and she said, "*Oh, I see what you are teaching. I need to go be with Him just to be with Him, don't I?*" The answer is a resounding yes. The primary need is to be with Him.

Prayer brings us into the Throne Room—into the presence of God. Silence is one of the best expressions of respect for God; therefore, it is proper to be still before Him—reverently honoring Him and His power and majesty. "*Be still, and know that I am God; I will be exalted among the nations, I will be exalted in the earth*" (**Psalm 46:10**). It is in waiting before Him that we gain the strength needed for a full life of service (**Isaiah 40:31**).

In this third study on the Model Prayer, the goal is to share various ideas and approaches to use during the time in our praying that we hallow His name.

23

For some, this will be a review since you already know and use these truths. Repetition can be the mother of learning and it is no burden to me to repeat them. You will remember Paul repeated truths as he wrote his letters and explained, *"For me to write the same things to you is not tedious, but for you it is safe"* **(Philippians 3:1)**. Throughout the studies, I will go over the same principles a number of times—and it is intended to strengthen your learning and understanding.

For a full study of the names of God, see my book, **Adoration: Prayer as Worship**, available by contacting our office.

God has revealed Himself in the Word—His character, attributes, essence—in a number of ways. One is through His names. We are to seek His face as well as His hand.

Confronted with His holiness

Until recently, my understanding of God's holiness centered on the absence of sin or unrighteousness in His being—*"God is holy and cannot look on sin because He is pure."* I am now beginning to see I have greatly limited His holiness. Holiness involves purity and morality, righteousness and justice, but holiness comprises more than these traits. God's holiness includes His "otherness" that sets Him apart from all He has created.

The word *holy* describes something that is set apart, distinct, in a class all its own. The term *holy* is a specifically religious word. Holiness is an unchanging attribute of God's nature. Though human beings and even inanimate objects can be described as *holy* when they are dedicated to God, absolute holiness is a quality unique to God Himself. It is the quality—above all others—that calls for a suitable response from those who come into God's presence.

As we begin to pray, we are confronted with His holiness and our sinfulness. As we approach Him, we become aware of unconfessed sin in our lives. Isaiah, the prophet, cried out in dismay and brokenness because of his own —*"I am a man of unclean lips"*— and his nation's uncleanness —*"I live in the midst of a people of unclean lips"* **(Isaiah 6:5)**. His response conveys both a sense of awe and an attitude of worship.

God has made provision—through the blood of the Lord Jesus Christ—for our sins to be purged **(1 John 1:7; Hebrews 1:3, 9:22, 10:4-14)** . God is willing to forgive us and to restore our fellowship with Him when we bring words of confession and repentance—*"Return, O Israel, to the LORD your God. Your sins*

24

have been your downfall! Take words with you and return to the Lord. Say to Him, *'Forgive all our sins and receive us graciously, that we may offer the fruit of our lips . . . '"* (**Hosea 14:1-2**).

The psalmist wrote in **Psalm 99** that exaltation and worship are appropriate responses to God's holiness. In fact, the last verse provides a clear motivation for all worship: *"for the Lord our God is holy"* (**v 9**). Without understanding His "otherness"—His holiness—there is no basis for praise and worship. When a true sense of awe—which only comes as we see God—is missing, our worship is affected, rather than genuine. We go through the motion, but what we are doing is meaningless.

The land of beginning again

If you have neglected worship in prayer or if your worship has grown stale, aren't you ready to do something about it? I hope so. Let's do it! There is a land of beginning again thanks to the graciousness and mercy God. In our next study, we will continue to explore the holiness of God as the basis of true worship which hallows His name.

Study Four

"And when you pray, pray like this, Our Father Who art in Heaven, Hallowed be Thy Name..."

Matthew 6:9

When God allowed His children to construct the tabernacle—a portable sanctuary used by the Israelites as a place for worship during their early history—He gave His servant, Moses, the pattern to follow with specifications delineated (**Exodus 26, 35**). No one can read the record without being impressed with the recurring statement—*"According to the pattern—Moses did"*. Moses *"was divinely instructed when he was about to make the tabernacle."* (**Hebrews 8:5**) Through His obedience, the tabernacle was built in accordance with God's instructions. God blessed their handiwork by covering the tent with a cloud and filling the sanctuary with His glory (**Exodus 40:34**). In fact, God was **well pleased** with Moses.

Later when God agreed that a temple could be erected in Jerusalem, He gave His servant, David, the pattern—with detailed specifications—for both its construction and furnishings through the Holy Spirit (**1 Chronicles 29:12**). What a magnificent edifice was erected by Solomon following the pattern God gave David.

It is significant that the pattern was followed for both the tabernacle and the temple.

A pattern for prayer

In response to one disciple's request, *"Lord, teach us to pray"* (**Luke 11:1**), the Master Teacher taught His disciples a pattern for prayer. Although the content of prayer may vary—even hour by hour—the pattern is fixed. It is important that each person who is serious about an effective prayer life follow the pattern.

Asking God's hand to move

Through prayer, believers are to ask God's hand to move in their lives and in the lives of others—which is covered in the second half of the Model Prayer—the "us and our" section. We don't have to walk alone. We need to ask God to move in our lives—that is **petition praying**. Then we need His hand to move in the lives of others—that is **intercession**. The greatest need of all is for prayer warriors who will touch earth with a focus on people and circumstances. Before we ask His hand to move and plead with Him to do something, there is something else we need to do which is clearly depicted by Jesus in His teaching on prayer.

What we have just described is PRAYER AS WORK; worship, however, must come before work.

Seek His face

A clear order is set forth in the Model Prayer. First, Jesus taught we are to praise God, then make our requests. Jesus told us, in the first half of the Model Prayer, to address the Father and come with worship—the "Thy" section of the prayer. What a beautiful model we have!

What a difference following the pattern laid out by Jesus makes in bringing peace to a troubled mind and joy to a heavy heart. In fact, many of the items which get on our "us and our" list will not be important anymore when our approach to prayer is to put our gaze on God and our glance on the problems. Praising God puts us in the right frame of mind to tell Him all about our needs. Too often, the first half of the Model Prayer is not included in our prayers. In fact, our prayers too often are more like shopping lists than conversations.

Attitude is everything

Man is finite—beset by limitations and weaknesses. God is **infinite**—with no limitations or weaknesses. God is **omniscient**; He knows everything. There is nothing He doesn't understand fully. God is **omnipotent**; He has all power. There is nothing too hard for Him.

What a mistake we make when we forget who He is and enter His presence without proper reverence and respect. God is not on trial when we come before Him in prayer. You and I are.

No excuse will cover coming before Him in a hurried, unthoughtful manner. Jesus knew His children's pressing needs for bread and for protection from the evil one could easily dominate our prayer time. So He taught, the initial approach is to *hallow His name*—as the entrance to time spent in prayer with the Father. What is it to hallow His name? That is the thrust of this study. Once you learn what it means and begin to practice prayer hallowing His name, it will make a difference.

Hallow His name

When we pray, it's appropriate first of all to exalt God, praising Him for His holiness and the glory of His kingdom. In essence, prayer is talking to God—not necessarily asking Him

27

for things. When we consider the greatness and love of God, how appropriate if the first things we say to Him express our appreciation and praise.

A proper understanding of His essence, character, and attributes becomes the very backbone upon which worship is built. Many Bible scholars purport that the basic attribute to describe God is His holiness. It is the key to understanding God—and our approach to Him. Do you understand God's holiness? In our last study, we began to study His holiness.

Holiness is one of the most important of all biblical concepts. Someone has said the holiness of God is like a tent pole holding up everything. When holiness is no longer there, or when people no longer respect it, there is no reverence for anything. In the Old Testament, the holy is that which is set apart to God, separated from everything that is common or profane. Holy objects such as the golden vessels used in the temple, holy ground, and especially holy people, were considered God's own and were to be for His use and service only.

God Himself is intrinsically holy. That holiness is displayed in two primary ways: in His own faithful commitment to what is good, and in His judgment of those who abandon the way of holiness and turn away from their "set apart" condition.

God exhibits His holiness by judging wicked people. In the punishment that Israel and Judah experienced, the holiness of God was displayed.

Without a glimpse of His holiness, one is likely to approach God at a level far below what is appropriate and right. The psalmist understood the centrality of His holiness and the comfort contained in it when he said, *"Great is the LORD in Zion; He is exalted over all the nations. Let them praise* [His] *great and awesome name—He is holy . . . Exalt the Lord our God and worship at His footstool; He is holy"* (**Psalm 99:3,5**).

Everyone should praise and honor His great and awesome name because His name symbolizes His nature, His personage, and His reputation. But the name of God is used so often in vulgar, demeaning conversation that most of us have long ago lost sight of His holiness—even those of us who are on the firing line of Christian service. Consequently, He is treated lightly in every day life by many of His children. If we claim Him as our Father—and He is—we must live worthy of the family name. We must respect God's name and give Him praise by both words—*"the fruit of our lips"* (**Hebrews 13:15**) and works—our lives.

28

For the Hebrews, a name indicated the character of the person named. *"Hallowed be Thy name"*—which means to acknowledge that God's name is holy" or "sanctified." To "hallow" is to make holy. It is to dedicate, or consecrate, to separate for purposes of worship. To hallow the name of God indicates that it should not be usurped by, or applied to, another. It is His name, His holy name. Since He only is HOLY, there are none comparable to Him. Isaiah quotes His words in saying, *"There is no God else beside Me; a just God and a Saviour; there is none beside Me"* (**Isaiah 45:21**). His character is His name; His name is His character. Sadly, most of us don't pay attention to the holiness or sanctity of His name. We repeat the phrase without really contemplating the magnitude of what we are saying. If we actually knew what we were doing—if we were at all sensitive to it—we might well fall silent in wonder and awe!

The ancient Hebrews were extremely cautious about using the divine name, for they believed that even pronouncing it put the speaker into jeopardy. The Jews looked upon His name with reverence and awe, so much that it was seldom spoken—only once a year, and then by the high priest as he ministered in the most holy place of the sanctuary on the great Day of Atonement. A piece of parchment lying on the floor or ground was never stepped on, for fear the name "Jehovah" might be printed or written on the underside. To the Jews it was a tragedy to desecrate so holy a name. What a difference in our culture.

The name of our God has been devalued around the globe. As a result we find ourselves plunged into a moral and spiritual morass like none the world has ever known. Our psychological compasses have gone wild. Marriages break up. Homosexuality is rampant. There is a surge in violent crimes unparalleled in history. The younger generation has been lost to drugs and alcohol and pornography has exploded everywhere. Secular humanism has become a recognized philosophy of life. International terrorism has come on the horizon. All our problems have basically derived from one thing—the lose of a sense of reverence, of a feeling for sacredness, of the conviction that there is a God who cares and has involved Himself in human life. The failure to respect and honor God's name lies at the root of all the moral and spiritual problems of our day.

We need to come to God in daily prayer aware of His power. The very context for the Model Prayer given in Matthew is a warning against praying emptily and voluminously as many religious leaders were doing in that day.

29

When we come with reverence for the name of God, we will gain the perspective and depth we need to have order in our lives. When God is honored, all life is sacred. When God is dishonored, nothing is sacred.

Hallow our Father

God's name is above everything. It is deserving of honor and glory and praise. And He is **our Father**. In essence, prayer is talking to God as Father in a sense of intimacy—not necessarily asking Him for things. Note the Father-child relationship which was the basis of Jesus' prayer life. Jesus Himself never prayed without addressing God as Father except on the cross when He cried out "*My God, My God.*" Again and again in the Gospel accounts, the word "Father" drops from His lips. You and I need to study the implications of the Father-child relationship established when we trusted the Lord Jesus Christ as Savior. We must hallow God who is our Father.

Jesus knew the scribes and Pharisees loved earthly authority and did almost everything for show and personal praise. So, He advised His disciples not to be like them. He told them not to seek titles for themselves, but to be content to dwell together as brothers or equals: "*You are not to be called rabbi, for you have one Teacher, and you are all brethren*" (**Matthew 23:8**). Then He directed them: "*And call no man your father on earth, for you have one Father, who is in heaven*" (**Matthew 23:9**). Jesus was not against fathers. He simply knew their inadequacy. He knew that no earthly father can love enough and give enough to suffice for all our needs, at every moment of our lives. Only the heavenly Father is equal to this.

To be able to call God our heavenly Father is the most audacious theological statement that could ever be made. Think about it—the God who created the world and cast the nebulae in space; the God who holds the whole world in His hands; the God who heard the prayers of the first man and woman on earth long ago and who sees the intricacies of the future; the God whose majesty is seen from the jeweled depths of the darkest ocean; the God who led the Hebrew children out of captivity in Egypt and spoke aloud when His Son, the Lord Jesus Christ was baptized, saying, "*This is My beloved Son in whom I am well pleased*" (**Matthew 3:17**)—**our Father**.

The God who fashioned the giant sequoia tree and plants the tiny seeds of pearls in all the oysters; the God who called Abraham from Ur of the Chaldees and made Paul of Tarsus apostle to the Gentiles; the God who imprisoned energy in coal

and whispered the secret of relativity into the ear of Einstein—
our Father.

The God who set the oceans rocking and shaped the crescent beaches of distant lands; the God who blessed the world with language and confounded it with many tongues; the God who ordained the very existence of mortality and then raised up Christ from the coldness of death—**our Father.**

When we consider the greatness and love of God—**our Father**, how appropriate when the first thing we say to Him hallows His name as we express appreciation and praise.

Summary

As we begin—in the very outset of our prayer—we are clearly instructed to glorify His name. His name means "all that He is." In The Model Prayer recorded in **John 17**, the words *glory* and *glorify* are repeated over and over. In the first-century secular world, the disciples knew that *glory* was "the high opinion of others" based on their accomplishments. They were to learn, however, *glory* in God's sight is never linked with human assessment; instead *glory* is linked with the revelation of God's majesty—which is taught throughout the Scripture. God's qualities are glorious in and of themselves. As we recognize His works, we praise Him for the qualities of being His acts reveal—and see who He is.

There is another dimension to *glorifying* His name revealed by Jesus when He said, "*I have brought You glory on earth by completing the work You gave Me to do*" (**John 17:4**). Jesus glorified God simply by doing God's will, and thus revealing what the Father is like to mankind. We need to glorify God by the "*fruit of our lips*" (**Hebrews 13:15**)—our words, thoughts, and heart attitude. We also need to glorify God by "*bearing fruit*" (**John 15:8**). The amazing element is that as you and I live in intimate relationship with the Lord, He acts in and through us, revealing Himself to others. Like Jesus, we can glorify God by being channels through which the Lord reveals His beauty to those around us.

31

Study Five

"When you pray, pray like this, Our Father who art in Heaven, Hallowed be Thy name, Thy kingdom come ..."

Matthew 6:9

Our motive in prayer must be sincere—to worship God from our hearts. The Lord Jesus Christ gave a beautiful example for us in the Model Prayer (**Matthew 6:5-15**). It is brief (in some translations only fifty-four words), simple, sincere, and unselfish (no "me" or "my"). It is direct, genuine, and reverent. It includes about all that one can imagine. It is all inclusive; it is inexhaustible.

The needs of God's kingdom come first, not our own wants, but there is a place—the second place—for prayer for daily bread and our other needs. Before we present our personal needs to Him, we should always pray first for God's glory and kingdom. The first three petitions center on the glory of God. The last four petitions are concerned for the needs of man. We need to include both divisions.

One summary of the Model Prayer helpful to one desiring to understand and utilize the truths the Lord Jesus Christ taught His disciples—and all of us who are God's children—is simple, but forceful. The Model Prayer deals with Paternity, Person, Program, Purpose, Provision, Pardon, Protection, Preeminence.

God's paternity

In previous studies, we have dealt with God's Paternity—*"Our Father."* We are not approaching a stranger when we pray. Rather, we are coming to our "Father." It is never necessary to apologize for coming or with the attitude, " I hope I'm not too much trouble."

A father welcomes his child's requests. This highlights the fact that we can come to our heavenly Father as we do to our own human father, with confidence and assurance that He is listening to us and wants to help us. God, as a loving Father, welcomes communion and fellowship with His children and delights in answering our prayers.

God's Person

The first concern of our prayers should be that God's name will be hallowed and adored. To understand who He is, we focus on God's Person. He is to be praised for who He is so we say

32

"*Hallowed be Thy name.*" The Greek literally says, "Let Your name be sanctified." In the Hebrew Old Testament the word *name* signifies more than it does in our culture today. The *name* of God is used for all the attributes of His being—His essence and His character. Although Jesus sometimes used *Abba*, an Aramaic word that children used, equivalent to "Daddy," Jesus brought forth the duty of reverence.

God's program

The second request that we direct to the Father about the Father continues the emphasis on who God is, but also God's Program—what He is seeking to do—"Your kingdom come." To pray for His kingdom to come is to pray that His sway be extended from heaven to this world (now ruled by the adversary) so as to extirpate wickedness. It is almost universally agreed that *kingdom* does not mean a "realm," but rather the *reign* of God. The main object for which we pray is the coming of the kingdom in the hearts of all men, women, boys, and girls. The concern expressed here is that His sovereign reign will be accepted by men everywhere, and that His will be done gladly and universally in the earth as is in Heaven.

The kingdom of God is past, present, and future. The kingdom came in Jesus. As we pray, "Thy kingdom come," we are seeking it in greater fullness.

Dr. Theodore Ferris, the late pastor of Trinity Church, Boston, as a seminary student was confused as he noted how Jesus talked about the kingdom as being present and yet something to come. An event in his life illuminated the whole matter.

In college English, Ferris took a Shakespeare course under the great Shakespearean scholar, George Lyman Kittredge, studying four plays under the microscope, learning the meaning of every word. Later, he became acquainted with a Shakespearean actor. Through him the plays came to life. Knowing all the parts, the actor would begin quietly to say the lines in a conversational tone. Ferris had known the lines, but had missed their beauty in the mechanics.

The poetry came alive through Ferris' friend. This led the pastor to begin work on the sonnets. Ferris began to reach out for more of Shakespeare, ever seeking more meaning in the poetry. As we pray, "Thy kingdom comes," we want His reign to be real in our lives in fullness.

When a person accepts the Lord Jesus Christ as Savior and Lord, the kingdom of God enters him. The kingdom of God is in

33

us (**Luke 17:21**). We need to extend the Kingdom of God in everyday lives reflecting the priorities of the King in the world today. The disciples were instructed to seek first the Kingdom of God and His righteousness and everything else would fall into line in their lives (**Matthew 6:33**). That is as true with us as it was those who heard the teaching.

A Christian should pray primarily for God to rule and direct his life in every aspect. The kingdom of God must begin in our lives individually. Our priorities in every facet of life need to reflect God's reign. What are your priorities today? Priorities are reflected in our schedules. A basic place to begin is to ask, "How do I spend my time?" To pray "Thy kingdom come" means nothing more or less than "Let Christ reign, here and now." When a time study is made, many genuinely born-again individuals are surprised and startled at how little of a twenty-four hour day has God first—or even in our conscious thoughts—and how little our lives reflect that Christ reigns in us. Some studies have shown that Christians pray less than four minutes a day if at all.

Each believer is to aim for Christian maturity (Matthew 5:48) as an overarching goal. A mature child of God concerns himself, not with his own plans and desires, but with the program of God revealed in the person of the Lord Jesus Christ—around whom the program centers and who is inseparable from His kingdom.

Too often our prayers are filled with our kingdoms, our causes, our plans, our reign. Most of us begin prayer with little concern for God's plans and much concern for our own. The next time you go to your prayer closet, begin by recording the time. Follow your usual pattern of prayer without variance. See how quickly you come to your own needs in prayer. I venture to say that most cannot pray one minute without bringing in "me or my" or "us and our" aspects into our praying. There is a reason for this phenomenon.

From the beginning of our lives, our natural bent is to seek our own desires and gratification. Our culture, through its process of socialization contributes to this aspect by teaching us to take control of our own lives and by reminding us to determine our own destinies. At the moment of salvation—when we accept the Lord Jesus Christ as our personal Savior—the Holy Spirit moves into our spirit. Remember the spirit of man died to God when Adam sinned and all who have been born since Adam have been born dead to God. Upon salvation, that which was dead has now become alive—we have been born again.

Immediately, a new believer comes under the command of the words—"*Thy* name be hallowed, *Thy* kingdom come, *Thy* will be done on earth as it is in Heaven." The problem is that self, which has reigned and ruled, is not eradicated at the moment of salvation and wants to continue dominating. It is obvious that a Christian—in order to effect conditions whereby he can pray what Jesus directed—must begin to learn what the demands are and how to live a daily life in accordance to the demands. A disciple is a learner. There is much to learn.

It is not natural to hallow His name or to submit to Christ's rule and reign. To hallow His name—as we have previously studied—is to live constantly aware of His presence. David understood this when he wrote "*I have set the Lord always before me*" (**Psalm 16:8**). That is the key to begin to move toward a level of maturity when our concern is His kingdom. Although we say the words, "*Thy* kingdom come," until we bring God into daily thought, word, and action—and become a vehicle for His holiness (which is what *hallowed* actually means)—it will mean nothing.

Our thoughts of God during a day tend to be fleeting and spasmodic. Spiritual maturity—which comes about by growing in grace day by day—results in our becoming more and more preoccupied with God and His kingdom on earth.

Before we pray rightly, we need to understand God's program—which is to exalt the Lord Jesus Christ—and consider what His reign is to mean in our lives as we live in an earthly kingdom dominated by Satan and his darkness. Until we have biblical knowledge of God's program, we cannot understand and apply His truths. Gaining the knowledge requires a commitment of time, energy, and effort—learning directly from the written Word of God under the guidance and illumination of the Holy Spirit who is a believer's instructor.

Start with understanding the meaning of the three words (in both English and Greek)—"*Thy kingdom come.*" The word "kingdom" is *basiliea* in the Greek which means "rule" or "reign." It is helpful, by the way, to substitute "reign" when you read "kingdom"—to keep the biblical perspective. You see "kingdom" evokes images of land and people, pomp and ceremony, and the like. But Jesus explained to Pilate, who wanted to know what kind of a king He was, that His kingdom was not of this world (**John 18:33-37**).

35

"Thy" means we are praying for "God's reign"—His sovereignty and rule which prevails in Heaven to come to earth. It is not a man-made kingdom for which we pray and cannot be advanced through politics or human government. Man-made kingdoms come and go. In fact, historians tell us that at least twenty-one great civilizations have come and gone from the stage of history. We are praying, therefore, *"Lord, do whatever advances your rule and reign"* on earth—"Thy kingdom."

What is the "kingdom" which was used by Jesus more than any other word to explain His mission (**Luke 4:43**, **Matthew 19:23-24**)? He spent all His time with His disciples teaching them the kingdom. After He died and rose again, He continued His theme. He appeared to His disciples and gave them commandments pertaining to the kingdom of God (**Acts 1:2-3**).

The kingdom was past, present, and future. The kingdom past embodied Abraham, Isaac, and Jacob—representing Old Testament saints (**Matthew 8:11**). The kingdom is present— *"within you"* (**Luke 17:21**). The kingdom is future—"Thy kingdom come."

The kingdom is not like what we are used to at all—*"My kingdom is not of this world,"* (**John 18:36**), Jesus declared. The kingdom is established in Heaven—where God reigns and His will is carried out completely and where His name is hallowed. The purpose of our praying "Thy kingdom come" is to bring His kingdom to earth in all aspects that He might put down sin, rebellion, and evil which characterize our day. It is to pray that He may take up His reigning residence in the hearts and lives of those who are in rebellion. It is a prayer for salvation—an invitation that involves repentance: *"Repent: for the kingdom of heaven is at hand* (**Mark 1:14-15**). Kingdom citizenship is granted when one repents and believes through an act of the will. His reign begins only when one turns away from sin to the Lord Jesus Christ—an invitation available for all men.

The kingdom comes on earth when we commit to the reign of the Lord Jesus Christ—as we bow daily to affirm His lordship and respond to the royalty residing in us. His reign is manifested in the believer as he allows the Holy Spirit to control his life (**Ephesians 5:18**) in all aspects which produces the fruit of the Spirit (**Galations 5:22-23**)—virtues for which we seek.

In every relationship, we need to seek His reign—with God as the primary relationship, with our partner if we are married, as a parent, as a worker in some job. During prayer, we need to say, "Lord, I live my life before You who knows everything. Let me reflect in all my relationships Your priorities beginning with my schedule today." His kingdom comes in my life when I yield to His priorities. The way I use my time must reflect His reign and rule in my life—that is the starting point for His kingdom to come on earth.

At all times, we must be aware that we are living our lives under His watchful eye. Whatever we do must document that He is reigning on our heart's throne. How easy to forget this in daily living. A little boy watched his father climb a fence to steal a watermelon. The father looked first one way and then another. The little boy said, "Daddy, you forgot to look up." For one wishing to let God reign, we need to begin our day—and live throughout the day—conscious that His reign must be reflected in all we do, say, and think.

The future
In the petition, *"Thy kingdom come,"* we have a request that the day will soon arrive when God will put down the forces of evil which are prevailing in our day on earth (sin, strife, war, suffering, sorrow, selfishness, cruelty, hate, injustice, greed, death), and, in the Person of Christ, reign supreme over the earth with His will being done as it is in Heaven (joy, peace, happiness and the opposite of sin's effects on earth). Specifically, we are praying for the day when our Savior, the Lord Jesus Christ, will set up His kingdom on earth and reign in righteousness—a day which will come.

Jesus was speaking about His future messianic reign on earth. The story of the Bible looks forward to the return of the Messiah who will rule in righteousness when the kingdom of this world becomes the kingdom of our God and His Christ (**Revelation 11:15**). Bible believers know history is headed somewhere because history is His story. At the climax of history, God's will shall be done on earth as it is in heaven—count on it. Based on the Scripture, we anticipate the day when angels and the redeemed will sing together. Before us shines that light; the darker the age, the brighter the glow.

When we sincerely pray "Thy kingdom come," we ask that the King will reign in the hearts of everyone now on the small bit of earth we occupy. The request is an acknowledgment that God has the right to rule all people—including us. It is to make our lives His throne. We dare not pray for His rule over others unless we honestly desire His rule over us.

We must be willing to allow God to work out His will in our lives now! The analogy of the Potter and the clay is pertinent. You and I need always to remember that He is the Potter and we are the clay and submit ourselves totally into His hands to do His will.

Learn to pray by praying

We do not learn to pray by spurts of purpose or casual acts of prayer. Learning to pray requires sustained purpose, much practice, and spiritual concentration. One can only learn to pray by praying. It is helpful to attend a prayer seminar and receive instruction in prayer. It is beneficial to read good books on prayer and listen to others share their experiences in prayer. But no amount of study and reading on the subject can take the place of actually engaging in prayer. As in many other areas of life, it is only practice that makes perfect. Consequently, we need to come not only in the spirit of that one disciple who approached Jesus for help, we need to come with the exact words of that person, "Lord, teach us to pray." Note that he did not say, "Lord, teach us **how** to pray." The only way to learn to pray is to pray.

Many people in Jesus' day made a mockery of prayer—which was a religious duty and one aspect of worship—by praying to be seen of men on the streets and in the synagogues. Their praying had no value. We are not to use "vain repetitions" or empty phrases since we are not heard for our "much speaking" or many words (**Matthew 6:7**). Effective prayer necessitates dealing directly with God.

Jesus said that a Christian is to pray to be heard by the Father. Therefore, one is to pray in secret. Every Christian needs a secret place to which he enters for a daily experience of closet praying—intimate communion with the Heavenly Father. Closet praying is secret praying. In Jesus' day, the closet was where the valuables were kept. There was limited access to the closet. To insure complete privacy, Jesus said to "shut the door." The word used here means not simply to close, but to bar or fasten. Such a safeguard not only assures that one is not making a display of his devotions, it provides the basic necessity for prayer—the shutting out of all distractions. In this uninterrupted communion with God, the soul is fed and the reign of God becomes a reality. The believer emerges clothed in strength and serenity.

Jesus was speaking only of personal or private prayer; He made no reference to one's praying in a worship service. Vain repetitions and long prayers are out of place and futile. We need to pray, not to inform God, but because prayer is communion with God and because of what prayer does for us. Prayer does not change God. He will never be any greater than He already is

38

whether or not we worship or thank Him. Prayer changes us and causes us to walk with Him in confidence.

There is nothing about life which is a secret with God. He sees our hearts, knows our desires, and tests our motives. As we live our lives, why should we strive to win human praise instead of divine commendation? God's estimate and approval are all that really matter.

A daily time in the Word of God and in prayer will make us radiantly glad and spiritually strong. It will help us to grow in knowledge and Christlikeness giving a plus to personality which nothing else can give.

Our study aim for these lessons is to consider our Lord's teaching on prayer and develop appropriate prayer habits for ourselves. It is important for each of us to understand the values in prayer and practice biblical praying. Why? John Wesley pointed out the reason when he said, "God works only in concert with the praying of His people." It is only through prayer that the fullness of what God's reign means will become a reality in our lives. Until individuals are born again, the reign of God is not going to be possible in their lives and they are going to experience despair and emptiness in life outside the kingdom of God.

A saved person needs to learn to pray if he is going to live the way God wants him to live. Many believers are living outside the will of God; the result is despair and emptiness—as characterizes unsaved people. It is simply imperative that we learn to pray—and that is the purpose of the Model Prayer.

A. C. Dixon, a Baptist pastor at the turn of the century, wrote: "When we depend on money, we get what money can do. When we depend on work, we get what work can do. When we depend on our own efforts, we get what we can do. But, when we depend on prayer, we get what God can do."

Study Six

"And when you pray, pray like this, say, Our Father who art in Heaven, Hallowed be Thy name. Thy kingdom come, Thy will be done on earth as it is in Heaven ."

Matthew 6:10

Why did God create man? More specifically, why did He create you and me? Why are we here? Where did we come from and where are we going? These are eternal questions which must be asked and answered if one is to have a full and meaningful life on earth in preparation for Heaven. Wise is the believer who pursues the answers to these questions and then molds his life around the truths he finds. Prayer is not getting God to do my will; it is asking that God's will be done in my life, my family, my job, and in my relationships—as it is in Heaven.

Two sides of the same coin

"Thy kingdom come" is asking that the King reign in our hearts in the here and now. The added petition *"Thy will be done"* defines the nature of the Kingdom for which we pray. *"Thy kingdom come"* and *"Thy will be done"* are two sides of the same coin. When we pray these requests, we acknowledge both the ultimate reign of Christ when the kingdom of this world becomes the kingdom of Christ and His every day rule here on earth now.

When we pray *"Thy kingdom come"* the thought is chiefly toward the Father. When we say *"Thy will be done"* we are thinking more of ourselves, His children. In the first we pray that He may **rule**; in the second that we may **bow** to His rule. In the first we say, *"Be Thou our gracious king"*; in the second, *"Make us Your willing people." In* us, *through* us, *for* us, *over* us, *"Our Father." "Thy will be done."* Is this were we are? Is it our will or His will that dominates our praying and our living?

Who is established on the throne in my life? Is it Jesus Christ the Lord or is it self? Once His kingdom is established in our hearts and He reigns, we want His will done on earth as it is in Heaven. As we study the Model Prayer, we can apprehend, but never exhaust the truths. Unless we resolutely maintain an attitude of mental alertness, we will lose our power to see, to realize, and to profit from His Word—and the result will be drifting. The picture of drifting is that of a boat caught in unseen currents and carried off course. As we approach this

40

third petition Jesus taught His followers to pray, we need once again to ask the Holy Spirit to be our Teacher—and then pay attention to His teaching.

Fundamentals

God has a will which He reveals to man through His Word. The Holy Spirit is active in making the Word come alive to the reader seeking guidance and direction according to His will in daily living. God has a will to be followed in every situation—even in the mundane. Each hour of the day brings circumstances where decisions must be made.

All of us have many days when we encounter situations we have never faced before which require decisions as to the directions we should take. This is the nature of life now, as it has always been—even in Bible days.

Paul and his entourage came to such a moment when their plans were laid out to minister in Asia—which was not the will of God at that time. Rather, He wanted them to go into Europe. Paul could not *"speak the word in Asia"* at the beginning of his second missionary journey being forbidden by the Holy Spirit to do so, nor go into Bithynia because *"the Spirit of Jesus did not allow them"* (**Acts 16:6-7**). Paul surrendered his will to the Father's will. The will of God was the determining factor not only in this decision, but numerous others in his travels as well. In fact, Paul said that it was by the will of God that he became an apostle in the first place (**1 Corinthians 1:1, 2 Corinthians 1:1, Colossians 1:1**).

Jesus, Himself, came upon such a moment of decision when He faced the cross as He talked to His Father in the Garden of Gethsemane just hours before His crucifixion. He prayed asking to be delivered from the cup of suffering which awaited Him, but added the powerful pungent, *"Nevertheless, not as I will, but as Thou wilt"* (**Matthew 26:39**). His purpose in living was to do the Father's will—even when the cost was high. He surrendered His will to the Father's will.

To pray that "the will of God" be done is to assert a specific life view which provides a basis from which to move out and face the world. There is a right way to live on earth; it is God's way. Praying for it to come about is to commit to that will, freely and without compunction. This makes the petition highly significant. As we actively pursue it with enthusiasm, our lives will be impacted—as well as the lives of those around us.

In the fourth century A.D., the church father, Chrysotrom, emphasized in his analysis of the petition that in praying *"Thy*

41

will be done" that *"we are to pray not to do God's will by halves, but to perform all things as He wills."* Thus, we need to understand God's will and follow it fully.

His will revealed

The essence of God's will is amplified in the teachings of Jesus recorded in what has come to be known as the Sermon on the Mount (**Matthew 5, 6, 7**). The Beatitudes with their ideals for Christian living (**5:3-11**), the summons to keep from murderous thoughts (**5:21-26**), to hold the marriage vow sacred (**5:27-32**), to be truthful (**5:33-37**), to love one's enemies (**5:43-48**), to pray, fast, and give with no display of piety (**6:5-8**) are some examples of His will. Other commands recorded throughout the Gospels are within the will of God (**Matthew 12:50, 18:4; Mark 3:35; John 4:34, 5:30, 6:38-40**).

Above all, the will of God is for everyone to be saved. In providing Timothy information to guide his praying, Paul reminded him to pray for all men since God *"desires all men to be saved and to come to the knowledge of the truth"* (**1 Timothy 2:4**). Peter expressed the same thought when he wrote, *"The Lord is . . . longsuffering to usward, not willing that any should perish"* (**2 Peter 3:9**). Jesus said, *"For it is not the will of your Father which is in heaven, that one of these little ones should perish"* (**Matthew 18:14**). God does not want anyone to be lost so Jesus taught us to pray, *"Thy will be done in earth."* His purpose is that men should know what His will is—and we are to so pray for that to come about. In praying for the lost, pray for the person by name. Prepare by mastering **1 John 5:14-15**.

His will amplified and illustrated

"Thy will be DONE" requires both <u>knowing</u> what the will of God is and the <u>action</u> required to accomplish it. There is no better illustration of one dedicated to following the will of God than the Lord Jesus Christ. He is certainly our Exemplar and Model for what our lives should be. The life and teachings of Jesus reveal the very thing we seek. He said, *"I came . . . not to do mine own will, but the will of Him that sent Me"* (**John 6:38**).

Christ, our Example, kept His Father's commandments He does not ask us to do something He did not do Himself. He only asks us to do what He did. He did not teach anything on His own authority. *"Then said Jesus unto them, When ye have lifted up the Son of man, then shall ye know that I am He, and I do nothing of Myself; but as My Father hath taught Me, I speak these things"* (**John 8:28**).

42

Jesus came to do the will of God and succeeded in what He came to do. He said, "*I have glorified You* [Father] *on the earth. I have finished the work which you have given Me to do*" (**John 17:4**). "*If you keep My commandments, you shall abide in My love; even as I have kept My Father's commandments, and abide in His love*" (**John 15:10**).

It is plain that keeping God's commandments and doing the will of God are one and the same thing, for what Jesus did throughout His life, He declared, was the will of God (**John 5:30**). Then He said, "*If you love me, keep my commandments*" and "*If a man loves me, He will keep My words*" (**John 14:15,23**). Jesus is teaching, therefore, that we are asking God to enable us to keep His commandments when we ask that His will be done on earth.

An ancient prophecy pointed out what He would do for us: "*Thus saith the Lord, thy Redeemer, the Holy One of Israel; I am the Lord thy God which teacheth thee to profit, which leadeth thee by the way that thou shouldest go*" (**Isaiah 48:17**). His will is to teach and guide us for our profit. This suggests that we may know when we are going in the right direction—and that is our need today. God has a will for all of us and we need to find that will and do it.

Further insight into what constitutes the will of God is stated by Moses when God counseled Israel what He wished them to do. "*O that there were such an heart in them, that they would fear Me, and keep all My commandments always, that it might be well with them, and with their children forever!*" (**Deuteronomy 5:29**).

Combining "*teacheth thee . . . the way that thou shouldest go*" and "*that it might be well with them*" certainly opens our understanding into what God's will is in the lives of all people. To fear God and to keep all His commandments constituted the will of God in the Old Testament (**Ecclesiastes 12:13**). Moses was to teach the people the way they should go, that it might be well with them. The will of God does not differ in the New Testament; neither does it differ now. He wants the best for all of us on earth.

When you and I pray "*Thy will be done,*" we are asking God to inspire, encourage, and help us to keep all His commandments for the same reason as of old—to teach us the way we should go, and that it might be for our good.

How important is it to do His will? The fact is that doing the will of God is a family trait because "*whosoever shall do the will of God,*" Jesus said, "*is my brother, and my sister, and my*

43

mother" (**Mark 3:32-35**). Jesus did the will of God. Those who are in His family must do the will of God, also. John noted *"He that says he abides in Him ought himself also so to walk, even as He walked"* (**1 John 2:6**) and *"He that does the will of God abides forever"* (**1 John 2:17**).

Jesus further reaffirmed this truth when He said, *"Not everyone that says to me, Lord, Lord, shall enter into the kingdom of heaven, but he that does the will of My Father who is in heaven"* (**Matthew 7:21**). When we pray *"Thy will be done on earth,"* we are attesting to the commitment we have to find and follow that will in our own lives.

On earth, as it is in heaven

Remember the earth has been the scene of six thousand years of conflict between those who do the will of God and those who do it not—between the forces of right and wrong.

Heaven is not a mere concept measured in terms of earthly value. Heaven is where God is revealed with the most impressive power and enchanting beauty, and where His will is done in creative energy, done within and without, done in all things in all ways. In heaven, His authority is supreme. There the motivation for worship and service is love. The inhabitants of heaven obey fully, delightedly, unwearyingly, understandingly, speedily, sincerely, readily, and concordantly.

What would be the difference if His will were done on earth? What about in national relationships? in homes? in your life?

"Thy will be done on earth" is a prayer that the world may be just what it ought to be. It is the very highest ideal of perfection. Greater thought never dawned, grander prayer never rose to God. It means: Let every nation on earth, every state in that nation, every family in that state, every person in that family, live so that God can bless with His salvation. The essential thing is that we know what to do and that we do it. That is how His will becomes reality on earth.

Conclusion

Before we bring our personal needs to God, we are to first pray something that is not easy to pray and mean it—*"Thy will be done on earth as it is in heaven."* Examine your approach to praying. Is it mostly centered on the natural "I" or "me" or "my?" This third petition of the Model Prayer points out the basic requirement of following Christ—self-surrender. Since self is always the last to go, most of us struggle at this point and are often defeated. It need not be so.

After sharing many truths about the superiority of the Lord Jesus Christ, the writer of the Hebrews expressed his desire for his readers when he said *"Now the God of peace ... make you perfect"* (**Hebrews 13:20-21**). The Greek verb "to make perfect" is not the one usually employed in reference to the perfection of the saints. This word is one that suggests the bestowing of complete equipment, the making fit. The reason we need the equipment is to do the will of God which includes "every good thing" needed to render service to the Lord.

The fact is that we have not equipped ourselves very well to engage in spiritual warfare. In fact, most believers do not know we are in a war and that Satan has wiles (literally stratagems to defeat our influence and our testimony (**Ephesians 6:11**). We live in his territory—not on neutral ground. He has under his command a great hosts of fallen angels and demons. His effort is organized. The hierarchy—first or head officers, staff officers, divisional commanders, foot soldiers—is actually revealed in **Ephesians 6:12**.

The intent of Satan is to *"devour"* us (**1 Peter 5:8**). The same Greek word translated *devour* here is translated *drown* in **Hebrews 11:29**. He seeks to drown our influence and testimony with unceasing persistence.

God has provided armor to protect His children from what our enemy wants to do to us. But you and I must appropriate it—which most have never done. The language Paul uses, *"put on,"* is interesting. It means you put it on yourself. The armor is there. He commands us to put it on. It is our duty to obey His command.

The armor is listed in **Ephesians 6:13-17**. There is the girdle of truth which is the knowledge God has put into His written Word. Consequently, believers should take advantage of every opportunity to learn the Word—read the Word, hear the Word, study the Word, memorize the Word, and meditate on the Word. Every day should find us with the Word of God open before our eyes and minds.

Then there is the breastplate of righteousness. Of course there should be holy living—a righteous lifestyle—but above all it is the righteousness we received from Him when we received the Lord Jesus Christ as our Savior. Put on shoes to carry us as we witness. Witnessing is a part of our protection.

The shield of faith protects us from the fiery darts of Satan. How much faith? When we have enough faith to turn to God, that is all the faith we need. The mind must be protected with the helmet of salvation. If we are defeated, it will be in our minds. The one offensive weapon is the Word of God—which is the sword of the Spirit. Once the armor is on, we are ready to go to battle.

For a complete study dealing with this area, you might want to order to a copy of my book, **Spiritual Warfare**.

However, we will never win the war if we do not know where the battle is being fought. Paul quickly draws us to prayer as the first activity mentioned after we have the armor on (**Ephesians 6:18**). How do we pray? Jesus has given us a model to follow—a pattern for our praying. And a part of this is to pray *"Thy will be done on earth as it is in heaven."*

The psalmist wrote, *"I delight to do Your will, O my God: yes, Your law is within my heart"* (**Psalm 40:8**). The beginning point for all of us is to desire to do His will above our own will and to want to keep His commandments. The bottom line of Christianity is obedience to the Word of God. To make prayer effective, there must be a willingness to obey, for that was Christ's example for us. To be like Jesus is our desire and He said, *"For I came down from heaven, not to do mine own will, but the will of Him that sent Me"* (**John 6:38**). In doing His Father's will He declared, *"I have kept My Father's commandments"* (**John 15:10**). In the beautiful expression of God's provision for our salvation in **Hebrews 10**, He summarized His life and work by stating, that the Father had prepared a body for Him and *"I have come to do Your will, O Lord"* (**vv 6-7**) picking up the statement from the psalmist. He used that body as a sacrifice for us—shedding His precious blood since the blood of bulls and goats cannot take away sins (**v 4**). Through His obedience, even unto death, the Father's will for a plan of redemption was effected so that every person could be made right with Him through the blood of His Son.

The death required for us to do the will of God is not the death of the will, but the death of our control of the will. Augustine, speaking of this prayer, tells us that it is another way of saying, *"Grant that we may never seek to bend the straight to the crooked, i.e., Thy will to ours, but that we and all doers, may bend the crooked to the straight, our will to Thine, that Thy will may be done."* It is only when you and I come to the point of yielding to the Father's will that we will be equipped to live for Him and bring others to Him. When we pray, *"Thy will be done"* let's start in our own lives. That will make the difference!

Study Seven

"And when you pray, pray like this, say, Our Father who art in Heaven, Hallowed by Thy name. Thy kingdom come, Thy will be done on earth as it is in Heaven ."

Matthew 6:10

When the disciple asked Jesus to teach the disciples to pray, He did not refuse the request. In the request, there is a forecast of Paul's finding that we have a weakness (the singular Greek word translated "infirmities" in the King James Version) in our praying: *"For we know not what we should pray for as we ought"* (**Romans 8:26**)—which is still true today. The disciple brought his request to the Lord Jesus Christ based on a perceived need. The disciples needed to know how to pray.

The instruction which followed the request was in the form of a Model Prayer—a sample, a pattern—because Jesus said, *"After this manner, therefore pray ye"* (**Matthew 6:9**). In other words, follow this pattern or pray like this. The prayer was not intended to be repeated rigorously through rote memory, but to be used as a framework or model. The prayer, only sixty-six words in Matthew's account, is simple in construction, comprehensive in scope, dependent in appeal, and only thirty seconds in length.

Earlier, Jesus had included the Model Prayer in His Sermon on the Mount as a part of extensive teaching on "how to" and "how not to" pray. In fact, ten percent of the Sermon—one of every ten verses—deals with prayer. Saying many words or saying the same words many times is not acceptable praying.

To pray is to open the heart to God as with a friend. In fact, prayer is a friend talking to a Friend (**John 15:15**). You don't even have to change the tone of your voice when you pray. You can use normal conversation. Such praying is not to be done in a public arena. Rather, our prayer is to be made in secret—shut in with God to plead where none but God can hear.

On earth as it is in Heaven

In the last study, we dealt with the will of God on earth as it is in Heaven in a general sense—to provide needed background. Have you ever wondered what the earth would look like if the will of God became a reality as it is being done in Heaven? We know that sin, sorrow, and heartache would disappear. There would be no crime, no war, no pain. There would be no more tears because the things which bring tears would vanish away.

In this study, we will focus on an individual believer doing the will of God—which is really the only way His will can presently be done on earth as it is in Heaven.

Through His Word, God has told us that His will is for His children to be Spirit-filled. Paul said that we should not be unwise, but we should understand what the will of the Lord is (**Ephesians 5:17**). It is crucial to understand that it is unnecessary for the believer to spend his days in frantic and feverish activity of his own choosing—which would amount to nothing more than wasted energy. Rather, he can discover God's will and walk in it. It is only then that His will is accomplished on earth as it is in Heaven as far as our lives are concerned.

Knowing God's will is of major importance. It is then that we can be what God wants us to be and do what God wants us to do—in a very efficient, effective, and meaningful manner. Unless this happens, a believer is not going to be in the Word of God, have a prayer life, witness, or be right in his giving. The path of wisdom is to discern God's will for our lives day by day, and then obey it fully. Few Christians live in the will of God because they do not understand what the will of God is. It is possible to carry on Christian work in our own strength according to our own views (ideas) and be completely out of the will of the Lord—a tragedy, indeed. Once a believer moves into the will of God as a part of his lifestyle, particulars will fall into place.

During the years of my presidency at Northeastern Bible College, chapel speakers often were led to speak on the will of God—which is not surprising since the mission of a Bible college is to prepare laborers for the vineyard in the areas to which they have been called. One interesting phenomenon was how frequently the speakers painted the will of God as something esoteric and difficult to find. I often wondered about the impact of what was being said on the thoughts and lives of the students.

You see there should be no difficulty in any believer understanding the will of God for his life because it is laid out plainly in the Scriptures. Without equivocation, I know what the will of God is for all of us who have been placed into the Body of Christ by the Holy Spirit (**1 Corinthians 12:13**). It is that we are to be Spirit-filled. Although there are always particulars of His will for us (what we are to do, where we are to do it, and

48

how), it is only when we come under His control in daily living that the particulars can come to fruition.

Spirit-filled
Being Spirit-filled is the will of God for each believer and we are commanded to be filled. **This is the most important command to a Christian.** Let me say it again. The will of God is that each believer be Spirit-filled. A person will never develop a meaningful sustained prayer life apart from living the Spirit-filled life. Unless this happens, his life will not produce the fruit of the Spirit which is delineated in **Galatians 5:22:23**: love—and out of love eight other qualities: joy, peace, patience, kindness, goodness, faithfulness, gentleness, and self-control.

What does Spirit-filled mean? The answer is found in **Ephesians 5:18**. It is important to write in your mind and the margin of your Bible in bold print—**DOES NOT MEAN QUANTITY!**—in the sense of more. Otherwise, you will be seeking more of the Holy Spirit and you already have living in you all the Holy Spirit that you will ever have.

Although the mental concept which the word "filled" evokes is "quantity" (in the sense of "more of"), that is not the analogy used by Paul. The picture is control. The verse has two parts and by studying this dichotomy the meaning becomes obvious. The following figures will represent the two parts of the verse:

The first little figure represents the first half of the verse and the second little figure the second half. It is important for you to label each figure. For the one on the left, the label is "drunk" and the one on the right "Spirit-filled." Why would the comparison between Spirit-filled be that of a drunk person?

It is easy to understand. When a person gets drunk, his walk and talk changes because he is controlled by the drink that is in him. When the Christian is Spirit-filled, his walk and talk changes as he yields to the Holy Spirit Who is in him. The result will be an exhibition of the fruit of the Spirit and the attendant qualities which come from having love reign; He will be like Jesus! **(Galatians 5:22-23)**

Just because He is resident does not make him president. It is imperative that we learn to WALK IN THE SPIRIT.

Fellowship with God can easily be broken. How can a person be filled? It would be unfair for a writer to challenge a believer to be filled with the Spirit and then leave it there.

Carnal Christians defined

Most Christians are carnal Christians which means self is in control—not the Holy Spirit. In fact, if you show me one hundred Christians, I will show you at least ninety-five (perhaps more) who are carnal. The result of this is catastrophe. Not only will war go on in a home situation between a Christian husband and a Christian wife, between Christian parents and Christian children, many times a church fellowship is wrecked because of carnality. In fact, a church in Kentucky split over which side of the church auditorium to set the piano on! Or someone will say that he has been offended and will never attend "that church" again! By the way, who told you would never be offended? The Lord Jesus did not! In fact, He said that it is necessary that offenses come (**Matthew 18:7**). Isn't this surprising? No, indeed. How does a person know what he has is genuine until it is tested in the crucible of experience. When you are offended and love comes out (**Galatians 5:22-23**), you know who is in control, don't you?

Why are most Christians carnal? There are two reasons. One is that most Christians have no idea about how to be clean and the other is that most Christians have no understanding of what Spirit-filled means. Most Christians think all that is necessary to get clean is to wrap all sins in a bundle and hold the bundle up to God and say, "*Forgive me of all my sins, dear Lord*" and there's never been a Christian cleansed like that! Most Christians think Spirit-filled means quantity ["getting more"] and do not have any idea about what it really means.

In the Upper Room discourse (**John 13, 14, 15, 16**), the Lord Jesus Christ gave final instructions to His disciples just hours

50

before He was crucified. He dealt with the two primary subjects which are basic to a meaningful walk with Him—the Holy Spirit and prayer. The key to successful Christian living (which includes Bible reading, prayer, witnessing, stewardship) is the power which comes from the Holy Spirit. It is imperative that a believer understand not only what Spirit-filled means as the will of God for his life, he needs to be Spirit-filled.

How to be Spirit-filled

It would be unacceptable and unfair to talk about the command to be Spirit-filled and leave it there. One of the problems for many Christian teachers is using the Word of God simply to tell people **what** to do without ever talking about **how** to do it. Although no teacher has the final word on "how to," we can be sure that when we use the Scriptures as the basis of our teaching, God's children will be strengthened. Remember, to be Spirit-filled means to be Spirit-controlled (**Ephesians 5:18**) which cannot become a reality until a believer is clean and yielded to the Holy Spirit. Let's consider how to be cleansed, how to be yielded, key Scriptures related to cleansing and forgiveness, and an example of a person who fell into sin and regained the joy of God's salvation.

1. How to Be Cleansed. God does not require a gold vessel or a silver vessel. He does require a clean one. To be Spirit-filled, it is necessary to CONFESS AND FORSAKE KNOWN SINS.

There are five points to consider.

a. **Conviction.** The beginning point in getting clean is to become aware of sin. Sin for the Christian has two aspects. God says (1) "There are some things I do not want in the lives of My children." What is sin? Doing forbidden things. What am I doing that God does not want me to do? Then He says (2) "There are some things that I want in the lives of all of My children." What is sin? Failing to do expected things. What am I not doing that God wants me to do?

Conviction means consciousness of sin. This is the work of the Holy Spirit (**John 16:8-11**).

Why are so few Christians convicted? There is a major problem. The Holy Spirit uses the Word of God to bring conviction and most Christians are not in the Word of God. Few read their Bibles regularly expecting God to speak to them as they read. Amazing insight can come from studying carefully one verse of Scripture in which God states what is necessary if He is going to look a person's way: *"To this person will I look,*

51

to the one who is humble and contrite of spirit, and trembles at My Word" (**Isaiah 66:2b**). Humble means dependence upon God—not self. In fact, the word **contrite** means brokenness. Until a believer is humble, God simply will not look his way.

How long has it been since you read the Word and trembled at the Word? How long has it been since you heard the Word and trembled, studied the Word and trembled, memorized the Word and trembled, meditated on the Word and trembled? Most Christians pay no more attention to God's Word than they do the newspaper.

The starting point of cleansing for many Christians is obviously to confess to God that we have not been paying attention to the Word of God. If a believer will come before the Lord with a hungry heart expressing a desire to hear from God, he will! May I make a suggestion? Set aside time to allow the Holy Spirit to bring sins in your life to mind. Here's how.

Get off to yourself with paper and pencil in hand. As the Holy Spirit to show you your sins. Follow as a model for your request David's prayer: *"Search me, O God, and know my heart: try me, and know my thoughts; And see if there be any wicked way in me, and lead me in the way everlasting"* (**Psalm 139:23-24**). You can count on ending up with a sin list as the Holy Spirit shows you what you are doing which God does not want you to do and what you are not doing that He wants you to do. Conviction will come and, often, it will be shockingly vivid and strong.

Conviction, however, is not enough. Many are convicted who resist or quench the Holy Spirit (**1 Thessalonians 5:19**). For those who sincerely want to be cleansed and Spirit-filled, there is a second step.

b. **Repentance.** The word **repent** means a change of mind based on new evidence. The attitude and act of repentance are absolutely necessary if a person is going to be clean. When the Holy Spirit brings an awareness of a specific sin, the believer must change his mind about that sin. Unless he does, there is no possibility to be clean. It would be an exercise in futility to go further. In the day in which we live, most Christians have not genuinely repented of sin; self is in control, not the Holy Spirit.

To those who have changed their minds about their sins, there is a third step.

c. **Confession.** Although the Bible teaches over and over the necessity of Biblical confession, most Christians settle for putting all sins together and saying *"Forgive me of all my sins, dear Lord!"* A general approach does not bring cleansing.

52

The word *confession* comes from two basic ideas—to agree with another and to say the same thing that someone else has said. Confession, which leads to cleansing, must be specific. What is the sin or what are the sins for which I have been convicted and have changed my mind about?

When my family and I were invited in 1973 to move from our home and work in Kentucky to Lynchburg, Virginia, to help get a new college going (now Liberty University), we were concerned about a place to live. Where God guides, He provides. Beautiful property came available on Timberlake Road (between Lynchburg and Roanoke) which became our new home. It had everything a family of five might want. The inside was very beautiful since the lady who formerly lived there was an interior decorator for Schwell's Department Store, the leading one in the city. There was cloth covering on the wall! We needed a place for Joshua George (Melody's cat) to live. We needed a stable for Mark's horse, Jitter. And there was a stable already there!

My delight was the beautifully landscaped and well attended lawn. It was like a picture out of *Southern Living* or *Better Homes and Gardens*. Many happy hours were spent doing yard work.

The first Spring that we lived there was another story, however. On a beautiful, sunny day, some friends from Appomattox and I were walking around in the yard when I discovered the lawn was no longer beautiful. It had been invaded by an ugly weed. My decision was to pull them all up, one by one, when our company left. Much to my chagrin and vexation, the weed broke off and left the root in the ground. I couldn't pull them up! When I went down to Colonial Hardware to see if there was any tool available to get the roots out, the clerks laughed at me, not with me, and sold me a forked tool which I still have today. Even with the tool, I could not get the roots out. You see, these weeds were dandelions and as far as I know the root of a dandelion is forever!

So, we simply ran the lawnmower over the root and left the root in the ground. Do you know what it did? Right! It came out again. This is what happens when one confesses generally—not specifically.

Is it possible to get the root out? Yes. The basis for this declaration is **1 John 1:9**. Confession leads to a fourth step.

d. **Forgiveness and Cleansing.** The idea behind forgiveness is lifting and removing a heavy load. When a Christian has unconfessed sin, a heavy load is placed upon him. He loses the joy of God's salvation as did David (**Psalm 51:12**). He does not worship well, walk well, witness well, work well or war well! When there is Biblical confession, the heavy load of guilt is lifted when forgiveness is received!

Someone asked me sometime ago if a person has to ask for forgiveness specifically in order to be forgiven. My inclination was to say, "Of course." Upon further study, however, I concluded that forgiveness occurs at the moment of confession. Instead of pleading to God for forgiveness, one simply needs to receive it. Praise the Lord!

The cleansing removes the sin from the record and enables the believer to start anew and afresh clean before God. The fifth step happens automatically.

e. **A Change of Direction.** Once cleansing comes, there is a change of direction. The believer is no longer walking the wrong path in the wrong direction. Sins are forsaken. Note that the change of direction does not take place until there is conviction, repentance, and confession.

It is amazing, however, that getting clean does not automatically assure Spirit-filled living. It is important for the believer to go a step further.

2. Yield and Surrender control by an act of the will.

God does not coerce or force. When a believer is clean, he is then in a position to invite the Holy Spirit to sit on the driver's seat. This is called "yielding." When he surrenders, there is joy unspeakable and full of glory.

Don't be surprised, however, if self asserts itself or Satan accuses you by bringing up sins that are no longer there. Since your mind is not born again, Satan can appeal to your own memory.

It is important to remember Satan does not have a place to stand unless you give him that place (**Ephesians 4:27**). *"Therefore submit to God. Resist the devil, and he will flee from you. Draw nigh to God and He will draw nigh to you"* (**James 4:7-8a**).

As you fill your mind with the Word of God, the Holy Spirit will activate any truth needed as you face Satan's assaults or as self attempts to assert itself and regain control. You *"renew your mind"* (**Romans 12:2**) by putting the Word of God into your mind—there is no other way. You may be sure the Holy Spirit will bring the Word alive as you heed God's truths in your daily living! Conversely, He cannot bring something to your mind which is not there!

Conditions must be met

The mind is not born again. Consequently, it is possible for strongholds to develop in the mind . Stronghold is a military term meaning where the enemy is in control and entrenched. A stronghold, in essence, is an area of sin which has become part of our lifestyle and needs to be broken down (**2 Corinthians 10:4-5**). What is the hope? It is to renew your mind (**Romans 12:2**) which comes about when you put the Word of God into your mind.

Some ministries of the Holy Spirit (our Helper on earth) become ours at conversion such as the anointing (**1 John 2:27**), the sealing (**Ephesians 1:13**), and the guarantee (**Ephesians 1:14**). Other ministries of the Spirit are conditional upon our obedience and surrender such as guidance (**Acts 8:29**), joy (**1 Thessalonians 1:6**) and power (**Romans 15:13**). It is when we meet the conditions that the Holy Spirit becomes the Enabler in our lives.

You and I don't have to be defeated! In obedience, let's be Spirit-filled! Spirit-filled means Spirit-controlled. A carnal Christian is a Christian where self is in control. A Spirit-filled Christian is a Christian where walk and talk is characterized by the Holy Spirit being in control! It is only then that we will **be** what He wants us to **be**, and **do** what He wants us to **do**! Let us obey Him!

Dr. Robert Witty, founder of Luther Rice Seminary (FL), and I have written a book on the Holy Spirit entitled **The Enabler**. In addition, a two-hour cassette teaching tape is available on the Holy Spirit. Both may be obtained by contacting our office.

Study Eight

When you pray, say "*Give us this day our daily bread.*"
Matthew 6:11

Do you remember the background for the Model Prayer? There are two accounts—one in **Matthew 6** where Jesus laid down the rules for Kingdom citizens related to their praying, fasting, and giving. The other is in **Luke 11** with a beautiful background set out in one verse. One day Jesus had been praying in a certain place. When He finished, one of the twelve disciples asked Him to teach them to pray (**Luke 11:1**). Jesus, the Master Teacher, knew that this was a teachable moment (a sense that the learner was ready) and did what the disciple asked—remarkable teaching indeed.

The result was the Model Prayer (**Luke 11:2-6**), commonly referred to as The Lord's Prayer. We have emphasized throughout this study that this prayer was not given as a prayer to pray routinely or mechanically. Rather, it was given as a prayer to teach us how to pray. It is helpful to a believer seeking to enhance his time with God to study the prayer—which begins and ends in worship and praise — and to emulate the teaching by following the pattern taught by Jesus.

Two distinct sections
It will be helpful to review what we already know about the Model Prayer. Repetition is the mother of learning. There are two distinct sections in the prayer which can be discerned by noting the pronouns used—*Thy, us,* and *our.* The pronoun in the first half is "Thy"—"Hallowed be Thy name, Thy kingdom come, Thy will be done on earth as it is in Heaven." These pronouns point us Godward and remind us to praise and worship.

The pronouns in the second half are "us" and "our." "*Give us this day our daily bread. Forgive us our trespasses. Lead us not into temptation. Deliver us from the evil one.*" After we worship, we are ready to talk with Him about our needs (which focus on **petition** and **intercession**). Most of us have the order reversed in our prayers with little or no reference to "Thy" and an overwhelming use of "us" and "our."

"Thy" section
While it is very important to deal with the "us" and the "our" aspect of prayer, much prayer is ineffective when worship and

praise do not have priority. It is one of those cases when "*you should have done those things* (prayed for yourself and others), *but you should not have left the other* (worship and praise) *undone*" (**Matthew 23:23**).

Not only did Jesus direct our thoughts toward greater and more valuable things because these things or desires are greater and more enduring, He knew that getting the mind off self concerns is the sure and only way to sincere and effectual prayer. His instruction aims at producing an attitude of mind and heart which releases faith. The most powerful prayers are couched in exalting God instead of self.

Praise, in prayer, does not change God. Rather it changes you and me. We are much more likely to trust God once we sincerely praise Him. Matthew Henry, writing in the early 1700's, pointed out that we can never add to GOD'S PERFECTIONS. He is already all that He can be. He is within Himself worthy of our worship. But how do we do it?

All prayer comes from need. You and I need to have time in our prayer lives to go before God with no other reason than being with Him—to love and to adore Him. The first purpose of prayer is to know God and to be able to worship Him rightly. As we praise and worship, we want to walk with Him and have the confidence to do so. Praise and worship changes us.

Remember that it is important to have a daily appointment with God which we carefully keep during which time we bring ourselves totally—spirit, soul, body—concentrating on who He is with love and devotion. It is helpful to have a place set aside as your prayer closet—a place as free from interruptions as possible.

"Us" and "our" section

With this study, we enter into the second section of the Model Prayer—praying for "us" and "our" concerns. The word *pray* as used in **2 Chronicles 7:14** and **James 4:2b** is the word *ask* when we want God's hand to move—God to do something. The elements involved in the "us" and "our" section of the Model Prayer are **petition** and **intercession**—not **adoration**, **confession**, and **thanksgiving.**

Petition praying is asking God's hand to move on the prayer's behalf—praying for self. It is from the Greek word *deomai* which includes a request addressed to God or man concerning one's own personal needs. The guideline for praying for ourselves is simple: WHAT IS IT THAT I NEED TO HELP ME

BE WHAT GOD WANTS ME TO BE AND DO WHAT GOD WANTS ME TO DO? Pray about it.

Intercession comes from two Latin words which together mean a "go between." Intercession is standing between God and someone else. In **1 Timothy 2:1** the Greek word is *enteuxis*—which means making a petition or request for others.

When Jesus used the pronouns "us" and "our" in His instruction, He highlighted the need to ask Him for whatever is needed—whether it is for ourselves or for others. Prayer is not only to include worship and praise—which is the purpose for which man has been created, it is to include petition and intercession. The four requests made in the last half of the Model Prayer have to do with the things man needs in order to fulfill the purpose. Jesus provided for soul (the window toward our environment) and spirit (the window toward God) and body (the house for spirit and soul): " (1) *Give us this day our daily bread.* (2) *Forgive us our debts as we forgive our debtors.* (3) *Lead us not into temptation.* (4) *Deliver us from the evil one.*"

Once God is given His rightful place with focus on His name, His kingdom, and His will, we have the proper perspective toward ourselves and our basic needs. By giving us our daily bread, forgiving us our debts, and by leading us, God hallows His name, brings His kingdom, and does His will on earth. Simply, the second half of the Model Prayer brings God into human life. He glorifies Himself by His daily provision on our behalf.

Bread

Jesus deals with our personal, daily needs. Both soul and spirit are provided for in the prayer. So is the body which needs physical nourishment to sustain life and bring Him the glory He deserves. Without daily nourishment we cannot fulfill God's purpose on earth. Above all, the instructions given in the Model Prayer are quite practical. Bread is the substance which maintains physical life. The first "us" and "our" request deals with food that is very necessary for the continuation of life. Bread is used in its broadest sense—not just that which comes from the bakery. It includes any element in any form of preparation that will supply bodily needs, whether it be grain from the field, fruit from the orchard, or vegetables from the garden. Bread means that which is needful to support the life of the body.

Someone has pointed out that since our daily bread depends on the successful use of the faculties and competencies God has given us to earn a living that we are asking God to bless that which we bring to Him to enable us to earn our daily bread. The teacher uses a toiling brain, the mechanic or musician or surgeon skillful fingers, the laborer strong muscles.

Some have maintained only bread for the soul is included in the petition. Their contention is that supplying the wants of the body is too small a thing to be worthy of being brought to Christ. That interpretation is quite unnatural, as well as unscriptural. Certainly if He numbers the very hairs of our head (**Matthew 10:30**), He is interested in the supply of food that comes into the home. Having made these bodies of ours, He expresses His interest in them by supplying what is needed to maintain them. This is illustrated by the miracles wrought to feed the hungry multitudes. He has taught that the body is a temple for the Holy Spirit (**1 Corinthians 3:16**). Praying for bodily needs is consistent with the Lord's actions.

The bread for which we pray includes everything necessary to support the various needs of our life in the world. It means all our physical needs. Our life is a compound of earth and heaven—dust from the ground and breath from heaven. Our prayer then should include bread for the body and bread for the soul. Bread is that element that gives and sustains physical life. But Jesus explained that we need spiritual bread as well when He said, "*Man shall not live by bread alone, but by every word that proceedeth out of the mouth of God*" (**Matthew 4:4**). That would constitute the Bible—which is food to supply courage, faith, love, loyalty, and all noble virtues and graces of the soul which make life worth living.

Martin Luther noted that bread includes "everything necessary for the preservation of this life including food, a healthy body, good weather, house, home, wife, children, good government, peace." He saw bread as all of the necessities, but not the luxuries, of life. What God gives us by way of luxury is His gracious hand, but His promise is to provide necessities. When we ask for "daily bread" we are acknowledging God as the source of life, shelter, clothing—the necessities.

Everything we have is from God (**Genesis 1:29-31**). He brings the rain to make things grow, cycles the seasons, and produces minerals to make the soil fertile. He provides the animals from which we make our clothing and petroleum from which we produce our synthetics. As He provides our food, we are to receive it with thanksgiving and sanctify it with the Word of God and prayer (**1 Timothy 4:3**). God is the source of

59

everything. Further, God is active daily in upholding His world so that it supports our physical needs.

Daily

We are struck by the word "daily" in this prayer. The Greek word *epiousion* is used only here in the New Testament. Bible scholars have given over thirty different explanations of its meaning—because the original word is found nowhere else, either in sacred or classical literature. Many believed that Matthew and Luke coined it to translate the Aramaic phrase used by the Lord. Now we know it means daily necessities. Not until the fifth century does the word appear again in a kind of account or cookbook where it refers to a day's ration. It has been found by archeologists on a shopping list of a woman who sent her servant to the market to get something needed, but just enough for that day.

Simply, we are to live our lives one day at a time. We are not to worry about tomorrow, but trust God for today. All inordinate worry about the future is unnecessary. We are not to ask for provisions for a year, a month, or a week. We are to ask for bread for today. Once a person understands the impact of this truth, he will find himself with a settled peace.

One has provided wise advice in the a little poem: "Better never trouble trouble Till trouble troubles you—For you only make your trouble double trouble when you do." We need not take our worries and fears to bed with us—leave them in God's hands. Don't borrow tomorrow's troubles—live for today. God will take care of us.

You will remember that God provided the manna to the Israelites during their forty years in the wilderness. Without divine intervention, the people would have perished. His instruction was for them to gather a day's portion every day (**Exodus 16:4**). On the sixth day, however, they were to gather twice as much to care for sabbath needs—since they were to do no labor on the seventh day of the week. If they gathered more than was needed for a day's provision (with the sabbath exception), the manna would spoil.

God told Elijah, the prophet, to go hide himself (**1 Kings 17:3**). During the next three years, He fed him one day at a time. He did not know where the provisions would come from, but he trusted God.

A cynic asked a little girl who prayed "give us THIS day our daily bread" why she did not ask Him to give enough for a whole year. Her pertinent reply was, "We don't want stale bread; we want it fresh every day."

Enough

This prayer for daily bread is a prayer that we may have enough of the common necessities of life to meet our needs. There is no encouragement to extravagance or luxury. God's sufficiency is always enough to maintain life in a healthy, happy, growing condition. He has not promised to satisfy our wants, but our needs. We are not to spend time worrying over extra things, but are to seek Him first knowing that He will provide what is needed (**Matthew 6:33**). His provision will always be on time.

If we are not careful, our hearts may clamor for more than enough of life's necessities. We are on dangerous ground when we insist on having whatever feeds our pride, meets our fancy, or delights our senses. We may be dismayed by God's response.

When the children of Israel were on their way to the Promise Land passing through the desert, God gave them bread from Heaven—but they began to long for something more than He was providing. With tears of bitterness and dissatisfaction, they compared their wilderness fare with Egypt's fare. They wanted meat to eat and God gave them flesh for a whole month in abundance, but it was ill for the people. So *"the Lord smote the people with a very great plague, and He called the name of that place the graves of lust: because there they buried the people that lusted"* (**Numbers 11:33,34**).

We would do well to ask only for what is needed in the sense of **Proverbs 30:8-9**: *"Feed me with the food that is needed for me, lest I be full and deny Thee ...or lest I be poor and steal, and profane the name of my God."* He permits us to ask those things that are needed for our daily lives, but only for what is sufficient for the passing day. For the unknown future, we must trust God.

Give

One of the basics of the Christian life is to remember our dependence is on God—not self. One of the obvious thrusts of the teachings of Jesus is that we be mindful of that dependence. Generally, we are prone to credit our own efforts toward frugality and strength in bringing temporal blessings—and to forget God's name, kingdom, and will.

Regardless of our station in life, all of us are totally dependent on God to supply our daily needs. The late Dr. B. A. Prabhakar, the coordinator of our prayer seminars in India, said that USA stands for the United States of Abundance—which is

61

certainly true when we contrast our bounty with many other nations. But whether we live in affluent America or in a very poor nation, we are all dependent upon God.

After mentioning how God provides for all His creatures, at the end of **Psalm 104**, the psalmist acknowledged that God is in complete control. He opens His hand and we are fed; He closes His hand and there is nothing. He said, "*These all wait for You, That You may give them their food in due season. What you give them they gather in; You open Your hand, they are filled with good. You hide Your face, they are troubled; You take away their breath, they die and return to their dust*" (**Psalm 104:27-29**). We are dependent upon God. God is the One who feeds the mouths of us all.

It does not matter which mouth it is or where the mouth is located. God is ultimately responsible for our daily food. The Bible tells us that God is anxious to supply our needs. Every day, God feeds the birds (**Matthew 6:26**). If He cares for them, will He not care for us who are His crowning creatures? Yes, He will!

For all of us there is the danger described long ago as God prepared Israel to enter into the Promised Land: "*And thou say in thine heart, My power and the might of my hand hath gotten me this wealth. But thou shalt remember the LORD thy God, for it is He that has given power to get wealth (Deuteronomy 8:17-18).* Further, "*He giveth to all life, and breath, and all things*" (**Acts 17:25**).

"Give us" is an acknowledgment of dependence—which is a basic element in the Christian walk. The sense of it is that if we receive it not, we shall never have it. Few wish to acknowledge such dependence. But without the help of God, none can provide a loaf of bread, much less produce an apple, a walnut, a potato, or any other food product. This is true for the poor and the rich.

Our dependence can be better realized against the backdrop of one fire, one storm, one auto wreck, one plane crash, or—in our day—one unrestrained fanatic whose actions bring the level of the highest to that of the lowest.

We are wise to realize both our dependence and who it is upon whom we depend. The One who sent the manna to famishing Israel is the One who sent a raven with food for Elijah and guided the living, leaping fish into the net of Peter. He is still the sovereign Lord of mine and mountain, field and forest, land and sea. He is the One to whom the Puritan fathers offered thanks with beautiful reverence for supplying their needs when in desperate circumstances. With deep, sincere reverence and thankfulness, we say, "*Give us this day our daily bread.*"

The evidence is abundant that God delights in giving. Always and forever He is guiding the sleepless forces that pulsate in nature—the drop of rain, the life-giving air, the penetrating sunbeam. These make the growing leaf, the expanding vegetation, the ripening fruit to enable Him with ever-increasing abundance to give "*seed to the sower, and bread to the eater*" **(Isaiah 55:10)**. Only God can change the bread into the nourishment needed to maintain us—and He does so faithfully. He speaks and the bread nourishes our body.

Us

We are not to pray selfishly. He did not teach we are to pray "*Give me my daily bread;*" rather, we are to pray, "*Give us our daily bread.*" We must be concerned for others. Someone has noted that over one-half of the world's population go to bed hungry every night if they have a bed to go to at all.

People are suffering and dying from the lack of spiritual food as well. We are to pray with the thought of constant dependence on God. Then we need to be willing to put legs to our prayers. Remember the test of obedience validates or certifies that we are His disciples indeed. The bottom line of Christianity is obedience.

Our

We ask only for OUR bread, not that which belongs to another. With God there are no favorites, No one should have more than his share, or get his bread from the toil that is to support another's life. Any laborer—high or low—takes bread which is not his own when he takes a fair day's wages for less than a fair day's work. Likewise an employer takes bread not his own when he takes a fair day's work for less than a fair day's pay. We are at liberty to ask for our own bread, but not the bread which belongs to others.

Trust as we march through our wilderness

The overall sense of this request is that believers trust in the Father as we march through our wilderness. It is "*give us our daily rations and send us on our way.*" Whatever we have as our daily bread is to be used in the Father's service.

Daily I should look to Him in prayer. Daily I should ask Him to cleanse me from every sin. Daily I should meditate upon His Word, for it will be food for the strength of my soul. Daily I should surrender to the Holy Spirit and walk in the Spirit in order to display His love to the world in which I live. There is work to be done and He has no feet but our feet, no hands but our hands, no mouths but our mouths. "Give us this day our daily bread" so we can serve you.

Our Father will provide for our needs today. That ought to take worry out of our lives as we sojourn. A. B. Simpson has written that we Christians in this age of materialism need to understand that God does not provide grace in one lump sum; rather, God gives grace to us daily—one day at a time.

During the seven years of serving as pastor of the Kerby Knob Baptist Church in Kentucky, I enjoyed learning many spiritual songs which spoke to the heart—not only the words, but the spirit in which the songs were sung. One that touched me deeply every time I heard it was "I don't about tomorrow, but I know who holds tomorrow—and I know He holds my hand." That is the kind of trust that is evoked by this first petition for "us" and "our" when we mean what we say.

Study Nine

When you pray, say *"And forgive us our debts, as we forgive our debtors."*

Matthew 6:11

Do you remember the background for the Model Prayer? Jesus did not originate prayer. His disciples, as devout Jews, undoubtedly knew the prayers characteristic of Judaism, but were convinced that He was able to lead them far beyond their previous experience in prayer.

Corrective teaching

Part of Jesus' teaching about prayer was corrective: *"Do not use meaningless repetition, as the Gentiles do"* (**Matthew 6:7**). He was not concerned that people avoid praying for the same thing over and over again, such as a parent praying daily for the well-being of a child. "Empty" or "vain" repetitions meant using words which were not meaningful to the one using them. Only when the heart is in the words is prayer meaningful.

A few years ago, during a break in a prayer seminar in Bombay, India, a young man asked an interesting question: "Am I sinning by asking God twice for something? Am I showing a lack of faith?" As long as a person has a burden and an unanswered need, he must persist in praying until the Lord sends the answer or the burden is lifted (**Luke 11:18**). "Ask" (**Matthew 7:7; John 14:13**) in the Greek means "ask and keep on asking." Actually, Jesus cautioned against growing weary and fainting in prayer—which indeed is easy to do (**Luke 18:1**).

Further, Jesus condemned prayer that was designed to speak to man rather than God—as the Pharisees were prone to do (**Matthew 6:5-6**). Since the closet was where folks in His day kept their valuables, there was limited access to the closet. It is plain that Jesus was directing that having a prayer place as free from interruptions as possible makes a difference.

Unprecedented teaching

Part of His teaching was unprecedented including addressing God as Father—something no person had ever done before. The basis of prayer is that God is our Father. Our

65

approach is to One who loves and cares for us. "Father" is the most important word of all. What is involved in prayer, anyway? **Prayer is to the Father through the Son in the power of the Holy Spirit.**

First, God's interest

In the Model Prayer, Jesus is teaching HOW TO PRAY—rather than what to say when we pray. We have learned that the Model Prayer divides itself naturally into two parts. In Matthew's account the first part is concerned with God's interests—and as such must always come first. It is comprised of three petitions that concern the "name," "kingdom," and "will" of God. True prayer has a first concern for the things of God—centered in "Thy" as over against "my." His name stands for His character. His kingdom comes in a measure whenever God's rule becomes a reality in a human life (**Luke 10:9, 11; 11:20**) and when God's own values for life and the world are espoused. When there is acceptance of the fact that God governs all life, God's will prevails. His will must begin with the pray-er before reaching out to include others or society in general.

God's will is done perfectly in everything in heaven, and so it must be in earth. Richard Baxter, the renowned Puritan minister who is remembered as the man "who preached as a dying man to dying men, and never sure to preach again," caught the thought well when he said, "Lord, what Thou wilt, where Thou wilt, and when Thou wilt." It is easy to forget God's name, kingdom, and will.

Praise does not change God, it changes us by producing an attitude of mind and heart of trust and faith. Jesus knew the reality of this truth; therefore, He admonished His disciples to begin and end prayer with praise. God is interested in us totally—our provisions for daily necessities in all areas including physical and spiritual. Rather than focusing on material things for personal use and pleasure, Jesus places honoring and revering God's name, setting up and increasing His rule in the hearts of individuals and in groups, and the performance of His will on earth first. He summed up this attitude by explaining the result of putting God first: "*Seek ye first the kingdom* [rule or reign] *of God and His righteousness, and all these things shall be added unto you*" (**Matthew 6:33**).

Quite simply, Jesus knew the road to sincere and effectual prayer is getting our minds off "us" and "our" matters and placing them on "Thy" matters—Godward, not manward. He directed our thoughts toward greater and more valuable things.

66

Selfishness and self-serving end when we focus on the One who is a stranger to selfishness. From an attitude of trust and faith, we may then ask Him for our actual daily needs.

Then, man's physical interests
The second part of the Model Prayer relates to the individual and social needs of mankind. It's right to pray for daily needs. In order to serve God's Kingdom and do His will, we need physical strength to work, a job (to have money for food, clothing, shelter, transportation, and other essentials). To pray for "daily bread" is to acknowledge a constant dependence upon God for all the needs of life. "Give us" is intended to make and to keep us always mindful of our dependence on God. It is not easy to remember that the strength and skill to earn a living come from God—and not ourselves. "*And thou say in thy heart, my power and the might of mine hand hath gotten me this wealth. But thou shalt remember the Lord thy God; for it is He that giveth thee power to get wealth*" (**Deuteronomy 8:17-18**). "*He giveth to all life, and breath, and all things*" (**Acts 17:25**). God's people do not live by human resources, but by the gifts of God. This petition is an antidote for worry. God's provisions are daily, not all at once.

Man's spiritual interests
Life is more than physical, however, and there is a place in prayer for the recognition of spiritual needs—especially those of human relationships that have become strained or ruptured destroying peace and happiness.
"*And forgive us our debts.*" "And" is a connective, the link that joins together two things which are important. With the same assurance that we ask for our daily bread, we ask that our sins be forgiven. "Give" and "forgive"—"bread" and "sins." Asking for bread is a daily affair. The conjunctive uniting the two requests indicates they were of equal consequence. Asking for forgiveness is also a daily affair. People make mistakes every day. None but God can make a grain of wheat for bread, and none but God can forgive sins. Man needs bread for his stomach, because without it he will die. More important, he needs forgiveness for his soul, for without it he will die twice over—not only physically, but spiritually.

The fact of sin
Forgiveness is necessary because of sin. We all have sinned and gone astray—there are no exceptions. We are all guilty and

67

cannot look God in the eye in innocence. Paul's statement, "*all have sinned and fall short of the glory of God*" (**Romans 3:23**) realistically reports this fact so graphically depicted in the Bible and so vividly portrayed in our personal experiences. If one were to disregard the words "sin," "sinning," and "sinners" in the Bible, the story of Redemption would no longer make sense.

Both the Old and New Testaments are concerned with the fact of sin—what sin does to personal relationships, how it comes between man and God, between man and man, and the need for forgiveness. The multiple references to the judgment of God, as well as the constant offer of the forgiveness of God, can only be interpreted against the background of the reality of sin. A society or a person that considers sin as only a psychological maladjustment or a sociological aberration will never understand the Bible—its message will seem unnecessary from beginning to end.

It is no accident that after the creation stories in the first two chapters of Genesis the narrative of the Garden of Eden immediately follows. The whole of the Bible is built upon key themes: creation, sin, and redemption—and forgiveness lies at the heart of what it has to say about the last of them.

While this study on the Model Prayer is not the place to examine all that the Scriptures have to say about sin and redemption, a sense of sin—which is so obviously missing in our day when men make a mock of sin and sin without blushing (**Jeremiah 6:25, 8:12**)—is necessary. Until a person knows he has sinned, he will not feel any need for a Savior. The cost of forgiveness was the blood of the Lamb of God—the Lord Jesus Christ who died in His thirty-third year on Calvary as our perfect sacrifice.

We are concerned with a single and exceedingly brief petition at the heart of the Model Prayer which provides instruction for a Christian's prayer life: "*And forgive us our debts, as we also have forgiven our debtors*" (**Matthew 6:12**) and Luke's variant wording: "*And forgive us our sins, for we ourselves forgive everyone who is indebted to us*" (**Luke 11:4**).

Sin is a debt to be paid

It was common in Jesus' day for the Jews to think of sins as debts owed to God. Sins were failures to deliver to God that which was due Him. Since the Model Prayer was given to teach God's children, we know this is a prayer for forgiveness by those already forgiven—thus, unsaved people have no grounds to pray in this manner. Thus, the word "debt" does not have reference to financial obligations at all.

The Bible never leaves us in doubt as to what sin is, or as to its seriousness. Sin has been defined as any want of conformity to, or transgression of, the law of God. Sin for the Christian has two aspects. First, God says: "There are some things I don't want in the lives of My children." Second, He says, "There are some things I want in the lives of all My children." What am I doing that God does not want me to do? What am I not doing that He wants me to do? Sin for the Christian is doing forbidden things and failing to do expected things. We sin when we do anything that God forbids, or when we fail to do something that God commands. Either one is sin.

Unforgiven and unconfessed sin robs the believer of the joy of God's salvation (**Psalm 51:12**) and closes down the prayer line (**Psalm 66:18, Isaiah 59:1-2**). Forgiveness and cleansing open the channel for both joy and prayer. Most Christians today are carnal Christians—self is in control, not the Holy Spirit. Have you ever thought "*I wish I had not said that!*" or "*I wish I had not done that!*"? Of course—we all have because the mind, emotions, will, and body are not born again and there is a struggle (**Romans 7**) which can only be overcome by Spirit-filled living which comes about when the Holy Spirit is allowed to control our lives—to sit on the driver's seat.

You will remember that the Model Prayer is a pattern for praying—a framework to guide the believer. It is necessary for a Christian to be on praying ground and that is impossible until he is clean before God. The provision that God has made for cleansing must be applied to effect even a daily walk with God. Although salvation brings about a bath which never has to be repeated, our feet get dirty as we walk in the world and need daily cleansing. Isn't this what Jesus told Peter in **John 13:10**: "*He who is bathed needs only to wash his feet, but is completely clean*"? JUDICIAL FORGIVENESS takes place at conversion when the penalty of sin is removed which is strictly a matter of grace through faith. That is the bath. Daily cleansing is washing the feet.

Forgiveness and cleansing

Forgiveness comes when (1) the Holy Spirit makes a saved person aware that he has sinned (conviction), (2) the person changes his mind about that specific sin (repentance), and (3) then says, in agreement, the same thing about the sin that God says (confession). Only then cleansing and forgiveness are

69

accomplished in the life of a believer: *"If we confess our sins, He is faithful and just to forgive us and cleanse us from all unrighteousness"* (**1 John 1:9**).

Forgiveness means "lift and remove a heavy load" [of guilt] which is best shown by the scape goat on the day of atonement which is described in **Leviticus 16:20-22**. Once a year on the Day of Atonement, the priest put his hands on the head of the goat confessing for the people all their transgressions, sins, and iniquities. Then the goat was released in the wilderness. The picture was lifting and removing the heavy load of guilt—which is forgiveness illustrated.

Cleansing means that the sin is not there any more and, for us, is only through the blood of the Lord Jesus Christ (**Leviticus 16:15-19, 17:11; Hebrews 9:22; Hebrews 10**)—not through the blood of bulls and goats (**Hebrews 10:4**). Words cannot forgive. *"Without the shedding of blood, there is no remission of sin"* (**Hebrews 9:22**). No one can give life who himself is under the sentence of death—which is the reality for all mankind. The possibility of forgiveness is completely out of the hands of man. Christ puts away sin by the sacrifice of Himself (**Hebrews 9:26**). God gave Jesus a body and He exclaimed, *"I've come to do Your will, O Lord"* (**Hebrews 10:5-7**) and *"By that will we have been sanctified through the offering of the body of Jesus Christ, once for all"* (**Hebrews 9:10**).

Both our salvation and our daily cleansing come about by the shed blood of the Lord Jesus Christ: *"the blood of Jesus Christ His Son cleanseth us from all sin"* (**1 John 1:7**); *"unto Him that loved us, and washed us from our sins in His own blood"* (**Revelation 1:5**); *"Forasmuch as ye know that ye were not redeemed with corruptible things, as silver and gold . . . but with the precious blood of Christ, as of a lamb without blemish and without spot"* (**1 Peter 1:18, 19**).

Metaphors abound to describe the extent of cleansing and forgiveness. *"As far as the east is from the west, so far hath He removed our transgressions from us"* (**Psalm 103:12**). *"Thou hast cast all my sins behind Thy back"* (**Isaiah 38:17**). *"Thou wilt cast all their sins into the depths of the sea"* (**Micah 7:19**). What a difference to walk through a day aware of cleansing—nothing between my soul and the Savior—and forgiveness knowing that God's hand is upon you!

As we forgive others

This is the only clause in the Model Prayer that has two elements and the only part which is commented on later

(**Matthew 6:14-15**). Consequently, there is no doubt as to its importance. Someone has observed that this is the most dangerous petition because the danger lurks so close that praying we lie, and lying we pray.

One of the basic requirements for answered prayer is a forgiving spirit (**Mark 11:25,26**). If we nurse a harsh, vindictive attitude toward others, we need not expect God to hear and answer us. We must forgive if we are to be forgiven.

Remember, this does not refer to JUDICIAL FORGIVENESS (which takes place at conversion when the penalty of sin is removed which is strictly a matter of grace through faith). Rather, this refers to God's parental dealings with His children. An unforgiving spirit in a believer breaks fellowship with the Father in heaven and hinders the flow of blessing. When believers are unwilling to forgive those who wrong them, how can they expect to be in fellowship with their Father who has freely forgiven them for their wrong doings?

In the Sermon on the Mount, Jesus emphasized the necessity for the forgiving spirit. In the original language, there is no time lag between the "forgiving" and the "being forgiven"—in fact, they are simultaneous. "Forgive us our debts even as we also forgive our debtors." Approaching God for forgiveness activates the conscience of one who belongs to God, and he will forgive others even as he is being forgiven. Forgiveness must be from the heart, not merely a matter of words.

One who has accepted God's forgiveness is expected to forgive others just as God has forgiven him (**Ephesians 4:32**). A forgiving spirit toward others, as well as faith in God, is essential for effective prayer. When a believer stands to pray—a common prayer posture among Jews (**1 Samuel 1:26, Luke 18:11,13**)— and realizes that he has something against anyone (a grudge against an offending believer or non-believer), he is to forgive that one of the offense.

This is to be done in order that the Father in heaven may also forgive him of his sins—lift and remove the heavy load of guilt. Divine forgiveness toward a believer and a believer's forgiveness toward others are inseparably linked because a bond has been established between the divine Forgiver and the forgiven believer (**Matthew 18:21-35**). If a believer does not forgive others, he forfeits God's forgiveness in His daily life.

You may say, "But you don't know what that person did to me!" It does not matter. God knows that life would lose its worth without forgiveness. It is necessary to forgive.

71

Remembering that Jesus was teaching the disciples how to pray, there is not here even the hint of human merit as the grounds of divine forgiveness as if people earned God's forgiveness by being forgiving. By the inclusion of this petition in prayer, Jesus emphasized that only the forgiven know how to forgive and sense the obligation to forgive. But forgiveness is a two-way street. Forgiveness can only be realized by one himself who is ready to forgive. We are never more like the Father or Jesus than when we forgive someone who has wronged us.

Summary
The Model Prayer is a pattern, a structure, a framework. Each point Jesus covered should be covered in our praying. The purpose of our studies is to flesh out in a usable form what He included in prayer. It is not enough, however, to study prayer. The only way to learn to pray is to pray. Now is a good time to check yourself to see if you are applying in your own prayer life what you are learning. Are you? My prayer for each reader is that our studies will make a difference.

Study Ten

When you pray, say: *"Lead us not into temptation..."*
Matthew 6:13

All prayer presupposes a sense of need—which is amplified in the sixth petition laid out by the Lord Jesus in the Model Prayer. True prayer is expressing absolute dependence on God. Not only does He have the power to pardon sin, He has power to lead us past all the allurements to sin that threaten His children day by day and hour by hour. *"Lead us not into temptation"* is a prayer of genuine humility and profound self-distrust in our human strength and abilities.

We are in a spiritual war—not on a holiday or picnic. It is important for us to understand the nature of the battle which is being fought and the role of prayer. Temptation is a real and powerful element with which every person must deal. All persons have their peculiar temptations to encounter, and surely need God's leading lest they be overcome.

Jesus and His apostles recognized Satan as a real person, the enemy of all souls, who goes about to seduce and mislead them. Since many people differ so widely in inclinations and temperaments, each one's strongest temptation may differ from another. Paul said, *"Lest Satan should get an advantage of us: for we are not ignorant of his devices"* (**2 Corinthians 2:11**).

Pardon of sin should not diminish our estimation of its strength nor our dread of it. When we have washed our robes and made them white in the blood of the Lamb, we should desire and earnestly endeavor to keep them unspotted by other sins.

Walking through a mine field

Someone said that life for the contemporary Christian is like walking through a mine field during a time of war—almost expecting at any moment to step on a mine that will explode and destroy one's life. Following that logic to its conclusion could make the Christian life one of discouragement, despair, and fear. If we listen to His Word, however, we are not to have the spirit of fear (**2 Timothy 1:7**). Fear is not to be our mode of operation. Yet, what are we to do when things lurk in the shadows to destroy us?

Temptations abound in our generation. In fact, I am convinced that no previous generation has been confronted with

73

so many things that have been arrayed against the lifestyle espoused by the Lord Jesus Christ in His life and teachings in the manner ours is. Our culture is filled with temptation. For example, our generation is overrun with sexual stimuli. The difference in past generations and ours is the avenue of the temptations. No other generation has had them piped into our homes in living color.

Every day, in our living quarters—if we are not absolutely and totally vigilant—the system of the world, the temptation of Satan, the darkness of the adversary come right before us while we sit at leisure, unguarded in our homes. We see the world system played out for us in such a way that we become desensitized to sin. Consequently, temptation is having rampaging effect in the church of God and in human society.

A map to follow

How is it that we are to combat the attack Satan is making on individuals, families, and societies? Do we just wait for the mine to go off? Do we walk through the mine field without any concern knowing that any moment it is going to explode and we might as well get ready for the disaster? Or is there a map we can follow which can take us through to the other side in victory—unharmed, unscathed?

When we read in the Model Prayer that we are to pray every day, "*Lead us not into temptation, but deliver us from the evil one*" we have the last two petitions which are required of us in our praying.

We have learned there is a "Thy" section in the Model Prayer. To pray in this mode is to pray for the glory of God in our lives as we hallow His name, as we pray for His kingdom to come, and His will to be done. Then, there is an "us" and "our" section. Having given glory to God, we are to come before the Lord with our needs. It is proper for us to pray for our provision—"*Give us this day our daily bread.*" It is proper for us to pray for our personal relationships—"*And forgive us our debts as we forgive our debtors.*" And it is proper for us to pray for protection—"*lead us not into temptation, but deliver us from the evil one.*"

Pray for protection

In this study, we learn that it is advantageous and very proper for us to pray for protection. "*And lead us not into temptation, but deliver us from the evil one.*"

74

In many respects, this is the most needful part of the prayer. At the same time, it is the most problematical—the misunderstood part of the prayer—for its suggestion that God leads us into temptation. Do we have to ask God not to lead us into temptation in order to avoid it? If we do not pray the prayer, will God lead us into temptation? Can God lead a Christian into temptation? Doesn't James 1:13 say: "*Let no man say when he is tempted, I am tempted of God: for God cannot be tempted with evil, neither tempteth he any man*"? Is this statement in James a contradiction of the Model Prayer petition? If that is true, why should we pray that God would not lead us into temptation when we've already learned in the Scripture that God cannot tempt us anyway?

Before we look at temptation and examine the mine field—and how we can get through it—we need to see what is going on in this prayer. To understand it, we need to understand the word for temptation in the text. The word for temptation in the Greek language is the word *peirasmos*—a word used over and over in the Scriptures. It is translated in various ways. It is variously translated "*test*," "*prove*," "*trial*," or "*temptation*." The word temptation in the English dictionary is defined as "seduction to evil." But the Greek word is neutral. Sometimes it means to be tempted, but sometimes it means to be tried—to be tested and go through the crucible of difficult times.

In the Model Prayer, *perasomos* has the meaning of putting one to the test or of being tempted. Sometimes it's God who puts men to the test in order to serve His divine purpose through them. The author of Hebrews viewed the temptations of Jesus in this light. They were to prepare Him for the office of high priest and to make expiation for the sins of the people. In bold, outspoken tones, he writes, "*For because* [Jesus] *Himself has suffered and been tempted, He is able to help those who are tempted*" (**Hebrews 2:18**). The point here is that the temptations Jesus faced and overcame were used by God—actually sent by God—to prepare Jesus for His final work which He is engaged in right now in our lives.

So, Jesus is instructing us to pray, "*Lead us not into trials, or testings.*" He is not simply talking about the temptation to do evil, but we are praying, "*Lord, don't let me go into a period of testing, during which time I will be tempted to do wrong.*"

Both concepts are tied up in this prayer. It is as though we were looking at the trial that is before us and understand there is an opportunity to either pass the trial or to fail it.

When we do not know what a day is going to bring, it is proper to pray as Jesus taught His disciples: *"Don't allow me, Lord, to walk into a situation today where in the midst of the test I will be tempted to do evil, but deliver me from the Evil One who in the midst of my test will take my attitudes and lead them away from Your will and way."*

Option to do right or wrong

In every test, we have the option to do right or to do wrong—to give glory to God in the midst of the pressure or to become angry or embittered against Him. Martin Luther had the correct idea when he said, *"We cannot help being exposed to the assaults, but we pray that we may not fall and perish under them."*

We will always have the mine fields and pressures. But we need to pray, *"O God, I need Your strength infused in me. I submit to the truths of Your Word. My responses, my attitudes, my thoughts are in submission to You. Lord, lead me not into temptation. But deliver me today from the Evil One who would take the situations of life and take me away from You."*

God's provisions

God has given His Word that we may hide it in our hearts that we might not sin against Him (**Psalm 119**). His Word prunes the branches to make us fruitful (**John 15**). His Word is the sword that defends us against the attacks of Satan (**Ephesians 6**).

A major text is provided to give us insight and confidence whatever the trial or testing or temptation we face—one of the greatest verses in the Bible for the Christian: *"There hath no temptation* [Gk *peirasmos*, trial from Satan] *taken you but such as is common to man: but God is faithful, who will not suffer you to be tempted* [Gk *peirazo*, tried or tested] *above that ye are able"* (**1 Corinthians 10:13**). You and I will never have too much of temptation—that is the promise of God.

Yet Paul's statement seems to be at odds with the Model Prayer. What does it mean that *"there is no temptation taken you but as such is common to man?"* Paul is not saying since temptation is such an universal problem that we should give up hope of victory and wait for the inevitable to happen—to walk into the mine field. He is saying the opposite. Since temptation is so common to man and is so subtle there is no hope for us except in God. When we try to walk through the mine field without God, we are headed for an inevitable explosion.

Universal and omnipotent

Temptation will get to every one of us. There is no person who escapes the testing and the trial. The one thing that binds us together in the human family is this—we all have problems, every one of us. No one escapes them. Our archenemy does not hesitate to attack or attempt to entice the most favored saint. All men experience temptation in one form or another and at one time or another. There is a constant struggle for the Christian. The more spiritual He becomes, the more refined and insidious are his temptations. A pull toward the grosser sins is not nearly as disarming as the drive in the direction of pride, compromise, and rationalization.

Nobody in the Bible escaped either. Look through the Scriptures and examine the commonality of temptation. In the Old Testament, read about Noah and his drunkenness. Read about Abraham who was a coward and lied before a heathen ruler. Examine the life of Moses who was disobedient—who struck a rock when instructed to speak to it and spent the rest of his life regretting it because he was not allowed to go into the promised land. Read about David, the man after God's own heart, who not only committed adultery, but murdered to cover it up. Look at Hezekiah who was ostentatious—Jonah who was rebellious—Peter, the first chosen disciple, who denied the Lord—John Mark who defected. All of these were men of God—men of great courage and accomplishment yet men who one place along the line succumbed to temptation.

I have been tempted. You have been tempted. Before you get too pious, I remind you that Jesus was tempted. That's what the Bible says: *"For we have not a High Priest which cannot be touched with the feeling of our infirmities but was in all points tempted as we are yet without sin"*(**Hebrews 4:15**) We learn from this verse that it is not a sin to be tempted. Everybody is tempted. Jesus was tempted. Sin enters when we yield to the temptation. Some believe that a really spiritual person will not be tempted. The exact opposite is true.

The experiences of Jesus in the wilderness furnishes a striking example of how temptation works. After a long period of fasting, there was an aroused human desire—the physical hunger for food. Satan suggested He turn stones into bread. It was not wrong for Jesus to be hungry or to satisfy it by eating bread. The wrong would have been for Him to exercise His divine power for personal gratification and self-preservation. Had He followed the suggestion of Satan, He would have failed

77

as did Adam and Eve. He resorted to the Scriptures to remind Satan that *"Man shall not live by bread alone"* (**Matthew 4:4**). Our senses are inlets to our heart. Inner desires such as hunger, craving for money, or for companionship, recognize no law of ownership or propriety or ethics in their gratification. Our knowledge and will must control, restrain, and direct them—with help from God.

Anatomy of temptation

A study of the anatomy of temptation will help us to learn how it operates and will prepare us for the onslaughts—which are sure to come. There is nothing more pertinent to our lives today than to learn how to walk victoriously through the mine field which is about to explode in every one of our lives. One problem is that Christians have a naive attitude about the spiritual life—that somehow if we have given ourselves to God everything will automatically be all right. We don't study, learn, or read the manual provided for us by *"Our Father"*—then we get caught up in situations we don't know what to do about. We are defeated and Satan has us where he wants us to be. We need to understand temptation and how it works. There are several steps, but before we study them it will be helpful to review the entrance of sin into the world.

The law of first reference is that the first time you find something mentioned in the Bible is the key to understanding it throughout the rest of the Scripture. The seed thoughts are given which help us understand the remainder of the Scripture.

Temptation today is the same as it was when it was mentioned for the first time in the Garden of Eden with Eve (**Genesis 3:4**). The devil said God did not really mean that she would die. Adam and Eve were **deceived** into believing that the consequences of sin were not as serious as they had once thought. He then presented something they could **delight** in— something to catch their fancy. In **vv. 4-5**, Satan declared they would be like God if they ate. Then came **desire**. She began to desire the fruit in her own heart (**v. 6**): *"And when she saw the tree was good for food and that it was pleasant to the eyes and a tree to be desired to make one wise,"* she wanted it. Then she **deliberated** on it. Eve was excited about this and began to play around with it in her mind. She ate, She was **defeated**.

As a result of their sin, Adam and Eve became discouraged and filled with despair. They were embarrassed, chagrined, saddened. It is interesting to observe the cycle began where it started—they tried to deceive. They were cut off from fellowship with God, stripped of all that God had given them.

This is the same pattern Satan follows today. The Bible tells us that we are not be ignorant of his devices (2 **Corinthians 2:11**). We need to understand that what happens in our minds is just as important as the activities in our lives because what we image or picture on the inward vision will ultimately become an actual fact of life if we do not deal with it there and cause it to be defeated. Now, let's consider the steps involved in temptation.

1. Deceit. Temptation begins with deceit. The first step is often the least obvious. We often don't even know it is happening. We are given the false impression that whatever wrong we do is really not that serious. In a very subtle way, Satan convinces us that our own desire and our self-centeredness and our determination to do our will as opposed to the Father's will are really not all that important. After all, Satan whispers: *"Isn't God your Father? Isn't He loving, forgiving, and merciful? What harm is it if you slip a bit and give a little ground?"* We begin to believe that. We are deceived by Satan as to how serious sin really can be. We will begin to downplay the seriousness of sin.

2. Delight. At the proper moment, Satan will bring something along that will cause us to delight. He will show us something on the mind screen that pleases and tantalizes us. He, in fact or in our mind, will bring someone or some situation in which appeals to our self-life. He presents a picture to us that causes some passion or some desire in our personality.

All of a sudden we have a low attitude toward sin and Satan brings something before us to catch our delight. In today's sexual society, it can be a person. At a time when society has downplayed marital faithfulness, you can be sure that Satan will parade someone or something across the stage to get your attention.

3. Desire. After deceit and delight comes desire. This produces a powerful response within us—a deep and compelling desire is aroused in our hearts. It appears pleasant, reasonable, very much to our personal advantage if we pursue it. We begin to desire it.

James, in the New Testament, tells us that one great source of temptation is our own human nature. *"Every man is tempted, when he is drawn away of his own lust, and enticed"* (**James 1:14**). Lust, as used here, is not sin—but a God-given human propensity. Lust is a passionate, longing desire, and eagerness to

79

enjoy. There are both lawful (legitimate) and unlawful (illegitimate) means to satisfy these desires. Desires are alive and aggressive and susceptible to the appeal of many variables: appeals of human applause, money, food, drink, sex, attire, and the like. When something from without arouses these cravings to push us beyond rightful means of gratification, then a temptation is constituted.

4. Deliberation. Desire gives way to deliberation on the potential of actually possessing that thing—knowing that experience. We play it over. We rehearse it. By the time we come to this stage of temptation, we have already fallen. Remember what Jesus said when he was interpreting the Ten Commandments that a person who lusts after another one has already committed adultery. Today, many speak of mind imaging. The way the mind is put together by playing something across the screen of our mind, it becomes in fact an inevitable conclusion. For example, studies in sports show that a person can practice his golf swing in his mind. We don't know the potential of mind imaging—what we produce in our minds. A person has already signed the contract to fail when he plays a sin over and over. It is not "if" but "when"—no longer able to differentiate between reality and what is in his mind.

5. Defeat. After the deliberation in the mind, defeat comes. We reach out and do the thing we deliberated about.

No sin is committed until the will consents to go with that craving and indulges in that one knows to be wrong, or to go from that which one knows to be right, and is enticed to do—either by omission or commission—that which one's understanding and conscience condemns. Then it is that lust has become the parent of sin, and *"sin, when it is finished, bringeth forth death"* (**James 1:15**). Willful and known sin crushes the conscience, deadens the sensibilities, weakens the will, dims the moral vision, and finally places the victim at variance with God. The cold word *death* certainly adequately describes that dreadful state which sin brings.

And that's not the end of it. The cycle begins again. We now practice the same thing that Satan did to us—we begin to try to deceive others.

Practical suggestions

Keep in mind that Satan does not have a place to stand in a believer unless the believer gives him a place (**Ephesians 4:27**). Satan must have the consent of our will to work his devices properly. Therefore, he is obligated to make his suggestions and

80

schemes look plausible and enticing to his prospects. He made his scheme look pleasing and flattering to Eve, and deceived her. *"And when the woman saw that the tree was good for food, ... and a tree to be desired to make one wise, she took of the fruit therefore, and did eat"* (**Genesis 3:6**). Paul said, *"I fear, lest by any means as the serpent beguiled Eve through his subtlety, so your minds should be corrupted from the simplicity that is in Christ"* (**2 Corinthians 11:3**).

The Lord teaches us in this petition, *"Lead us not into temptation"* that we should dread and shun temptation—shun the very appearance of evil. Paul told us to avoid unnecessary temptation (**1 Thessalonians 5:22**). We are to avoid going too close to the precipice. We are not to pitch our tents toward Sodom. We are to implore God's direction and leadership to keep us from the objects which would prevail upon us to commit sin and to keep us from becoming entangled in webs of danger and in difficulties which might overcome us. It is our duty— after being forgiven of sin—not only to keep ourselves from subsequent sins, but to keep ourselves from too strong a temptation to sin. When we lodge and entertain temptation in our heart, we are in imminent danger of becoming overcome by it.

Lead us

To pray *"Lead us"* is to acknowledge there is a Leader and that we are conscious of weakness and our need for His aid. The Leader is *"Our Father."* None other knows the way. Life is a journey through time, not space. Regardless of what we may have seen or where we have been, we have not looked upon tomorrow. A map or atlas will not help. *"Our Father"*—to whom we pray—knows for He sees the end from the beginning. Prayer is not a shout sent forth to someone in the distance. He is not a God afar off—but is every moment within hearing distance ready to reach forth His hand to lead us through the mine field.

To know clearly our need of God's assistance is a strength. Without Christ, we can do nothing (**John 15:5**). With Christ, we can do everything that needs to be done and be victorious. Paul, from his experience of appropriating God's strength, said, *"I can do all things through Christ which strengtheneth me"* (**Philippians 4:13**). To recognize and acknowledge our weakness and need of help places us in line for God's unlimited power. To pray sincerely, *"Lead us,"* expresses confidence in our Father's ability to lead us in and through the mine fields— through all the trials and circumstances of everyday life.

Here are some principles to guide us in the area of temptation.

One, request help in advance. *"Watch and pray that ye enter not into temptation. The spirit is willing, but the flesh is weak"* (**Matthew 26:41**). Make a previous commitment before temptation ever comes—ask for the grace of God. *"I know today there are mine fields Satan has set out to defeat me. God, don't let me walk in that way."*

Two, retreat from certain kinds of temptation. Remember Joseph left his coat behind (**Genesis 39:12**). There are certain kinds of temptation that we should not even attempt to combat. We are told to run from idolatry (**1 Corinthians 10:14**). There is something so insidious that we are to run. We are told to flee from youthful lusts (**2 Timothy 2:22**) and immorality (**1 Corinthians 6:18**). Sexual sin is not something we are to do battle with, we are to run. After the process goes a certain way, even Scriptures will be set aside. Therefore, we must physically remove ourselves.

Third, remove any means of sin far from you. Paul directed: *"Put you on the Lord Jesus Christ and make not provision for the flesh"* (**Romans 13:14**). Don't walk in paths or engage in activities the Devil has used to entrap you previously. Go so far as to remove from your life things that tempt you. We need to separate from things which entice us to sin. In **Acts 19** the Lord was working—folks were being saved and good things happened. His Name was confessed and magnified. Books were brought together and burned—which were involved in curious arts in the old life. They burned the things which would cause temptation. Do whatever you need to do to remove from your life the instruments used by Satan to entice you. What you read is an example. When you play things in your mind, you are on your way to defeat. You might not be able to keep sin from knocking, but you don't have to get up and open the door!

The garbage on the television entices you to do evil—brings the threshold of sin lower and lower as behavior unacceptable to the Word of God is played. In living color, your level of acceptability becomes lower and lower. If you can't turn it off, throw it out—remove the provision of the flesh out of your life. When we venture on Satan's ground, we have no assurance of protection from his powers.

Four, replace bad influence with good influence. Get into church. Get into the Word. Develop a daily prayer life. Read good books. Watch good programs. Develop Christian friendships.

Five, <u>resist the devil and he will flee from you</u> (**James 4:7b**). This will be our next major study.

Six, <u>refuse to live on the low road.</u> Don't try to live as close to the world as you can. God says in His Word that we are to live as close to Him as we can.

Seven, <u>be willing to be led</u>. We are never alone when we face testings or trials and will never be helpless against them. He will always—with the temptation or test or trial—provide the strength for a way out. Jesus said, *"Lo, I am with you alway"* (**Matthew 28:20**). David, speaking of the Lord as a Shepherd, said, *"He leadeth me in the paths of righteousness"* (**Psalm 23:3**). To pray this petition is to pledge our loyalty and co-operation with Him in leading us. Leading not only involves the element of time, but also our will to follow His leading. He cannot lead us against our will. Jesus said, *"If any man WILL come after Me, let him deny himself, and take up his cross, and follow Me"* (**Matthew 16:24**)—thereby acknowledging His helplessness to lead us until we become willing to be led and choose to follow. *"Lead us"* is to say, *"Father, I wish Your leadership and now pledge to follow at Your will and direction, to the very best of my understanding. I will bring my desires into subjection to and in harmony with Your will."* It is dishonest and insincere to ask God with our lips to lead us while we are unwilling to follow His leading—all His leading, not just some favorable portion of it. We must be willing to take whatever correction of thought, attitude, and desire necessary to follow His direction.

Prayer—a mighty weapon

An often proven truth is that *"God's Word will keep you from sin, or sin will keep you from God's Word."* It is also true that *"prayer will keep you from sin, or sin will keep you from prayer."* This petition—*"Lead us not into temptation, but deliver us from evil"* is above all a reminder of the mighty weapon prayer is in our struggle against sin. We don't have to be defeated if we lean and rely on God's promises and provisions.

To be tempted is to be honored

It has been well said that spiritual believers are honored with warfare in the front-line trenches. There the fiercest pressure of the enemy is felt, but they also are privileged to witness the enemy's crushing defeat. So abundant is the power of God. And thus highly is the believer honored. It is not true that the closer you walk with God, the less you will feel Satan's pressure. The closer you walk with God the more you will feel the intense pressure of Satan coming against you. When you are in the front-line trenches serving God, the mine fields will be there ready to explode at every moment. But God is faithful and He will not suffer you to be tempted above that you are able. So every day we pray, "*O God, lead me not into temptation. Don't put me in a time of testing beyond my capacity in the Spirit—but deliver me from the Evil One.*"

Deliver from the Evil One

"*Lead me not into temptation, Lord. Help me to understand what Satan is all about.*" In the next study, we will study the second part related to temptation—"deliver me from the Evil One."

Study Eleven

And when you pray, say, *"deliver us from evil."*

Matthew 6:33

How do you feel about the progress you are making in your Christian life at this point? How long have you been a Christian? Have you grown *"in grace and in the knowledge of our Lord and Savior Jesus Christ"* (**2 Peter 3:18**)? How like Jesus are you in your thoughts and actions? Is your mind usually on things of earth or things of Heaven?

A major goal of the prayer seminar ministry is to encourage believers to spend time each day in the Word of God. Are you doing that? God speaks through His Word. We read God's Word to hear from Him. After we hear from Him, we need to do something about it. Application of the Scripture leads to Christian maturity. Learning truths about prayer is important. But the key is to apply the truths. The only way to learn to pray is to pray.

In learning theory, a general principle is "use it or lose it." While the focus on these studies is the content of the Model Prayer as laid out by the Lord Jesus Christ, I strongly urge you to be alert to putting what you learn into practice. Mastering the information is not enough; we must use what we learn.

Review

There is no substitute for review of material already learned. What thoughts come to your mind when you go over the Model Prayer? I have found it helpful to ask key questions related to what I am studying. What insights have I gained about how to structure my daily prayer time? Have I made changes as I have studied the material and gained insights the Holy Spirit has taught me? Are there additional changes I need to make even now?

From the Model Prayer, we have learned to focus on God Himself as we begin our time with Him. It is proper to commence with praise and worship before directing requests for self and others. Another way to say this is that prayer should be "Godward" before it is "manward"—which is usually the opposite of how the ordinary believer structures his prayer time. Praise, of course, does not change God or make Him any greater than He already is; praise changes us and causes us to want to walk with Him and please Him.

85

The use of "our" rather than "me" or "my" is another overall lesson to learn. You and I are not alone; rather, we are in a family. While it is proper and right to pray for ourselves, it is equally right to remember others. A review of what we have learned reminds us that we are to pray for both physical needs— *"give us this day our daily bread"*—and spiritual needs—*"forgive us our trespasses."*

As you study, it will be helpful to think of ways that you can remember the truths you are learning and be changed by them. Remember comes from a root meaning "to imprint" and conveys the idea of "etching indelibly on the mind." It should be our goal as we learn to be forever changed by the truths we learn. The opposite is forget. There are many warnings throughout the Scripture that we are not to forget. The reminders not to forget obviously are based on the fact that it is in reality very easy to forget. When I preached my very first sermon as a seventeen-year old in 1953, my Scripture text was *"Beware that you do not forget the Lord your God"* (**Deuteronomy 8:11**).

Petition praying

Each of us knows that we should pray for ourselves. The Greek word *deomai* is the word translated petition which includes a request addressed to God or man. It refers to asking someone to do something for you—making a request for yourself. It is not only right to pray for yourself, it is crucial that you do so. You and I do not have to walk alone. When we approach our Father, we need never have the attitude, "Father, I hope I am not too much bother or too much trouble." You and I are instructed to come *"boldly before the throne of grace that we may obtain mercy and find grace to help in time of need"* (**Hebrews 4:16**).

Paul's assurance that God's faithfulness will see that we will not be called upon to bear impossible burdens encourages us— *"No temptation has overtaken you that is not common to man. God is faithful and will not let you be tempted beyond your strength, but with the temptation will also provide the way of escape that you may be able to endure it"* (**1 Corinthians 10:13**). Through prayer, we come under His promise for provisions.

"Deliver us from evil"

We should pray daily to be kept from evil as Jesus clearly taught in the Model Prayer, His guide for our praying. Remember the purpose of the prayer is to teach us how to approach the Father in prayer. It is not intended to be used routinely verbatim.

The words "deliver us from evil" are sometimes regarded as a separate petition. But they may also be considered as an explication of the words "lead us not into temptation," similar to "Thy kingdom come" which is followed by "Thy will be done in earth as it is in Heaven."

In this light, it is helpful to keep in mind the previous study which dealt with "*Lead us not into temptation.*" Although temptation includes trials intended to make us grow in dependence upon the Lord and not ourselves, it also embraces the pull upon us to do wrong.

The prayer is not that we be housed and protected against temptation, but that we can be given strength to meet it. To be delivered from evil means that men shall not be overwhelmed in the tempting hour.

In a sense, here is what we are saying: May we not be found in a situation beyond our power to handle. But if we are, may we count on God's power and support to deliver us—enabling us to overcome.

Jabez's prayer

Does the petition *"keep me from evil"* sound familiar? If you have been in a prayer seminar, it should. During a prayer seminar, the prayer of Jabez (**1 Chronicles 4:9-10**) is used as an Old Testament example of petition praying—praying for oneself. Included in his instructive prayer is a request that parallels what Jesus is teaching, "*Keep me from evil that it may not grieve me.*" Isn't this what Jesus was teaching?

Sin robs the Christian of the joy of God's salvation as illustrated in the experience of King David, a person described as a "*man after God's own heart*" (**1 Samuel 13:14, Acts 13:22**). The sweet singer of Israel allowed sin to enter his life. The consequence was to lose the joy of God's salvation (**Psalm 51:12**). When there is unconfessed, unforsaken sin, a Christian does not worship well, walk well, witness well, work well, or war well.

Two exegeses

We are to ask for divine help to be kept from evil or to be kept from the evil one. In a number of English translations, the words "*keep us from evil*" are found. Other translations are "*keep us from the evil one.*" In Greek, the genitive *tou ponerous* can be either neuter or masculine. If it is neuter, the translation is "*from evil.*" If it is masculine, it should read "*from the evil one.*" "From evil" would be a general reference from all evil. "From the evil one" would suggest a personal source of evil. The evil one is the devil or other representatives of the source of evil in personal terms. Actually, I believe it is proper to include both elements in the request. Both the evil that is in this world and the evil one are realities we dare not ignore.

The reality of evil

It is necessary that we be brought to see and to hate evil that we may earnestly desire to be delivered from it. As long as evil is likely to come between us and our Father, we need to pray "*deliver us from evil.*" Evil is at work in the world as it has been since Satan was cast out of Heaven. We pray to God because there is evil within us and all around us and we can do nothing without God's help. Evil is any thing which disturbs our peace with God and hinders our relationship and communication with Him. Things which are not evil in themselves may become evil when they begin to dim our vision of our Father's face or to dampen our ardor or zeal for His cause. Thus, evil often lurks in things very close to us—jobs, possessions, the culture in which we live—and people around us—family members, friends, acquaintances, work mates. Remember, we have previously pointed out that for most Christians, a pull toward grosser sins is not nearly so disarming as the drive in the direction of pride, compromise, and rationalization. Think about it.

To pray sincerely that the Lord deliver us from evil is to ask that He keep us from the subtle schemes of Satan which may overcome us and separate us from that which is pure and wholesome, and from the favor of our Father. It is to ask that He deliver us from all evil attacks along the way He leads us—from the evils of the spirit as well as the evils of the flesh.

The reality of Satan

The Christian has an enemy who constantly works to defeat the cause of the Lord Jesus Christ. Satan is alive and well on earth destroying the work of the Lord Jesus Christ whenever he can. To do this, he attacks God's children in an effort to nullify their influence. In fact, Peter reminds believers to "*be self-controlled and alert. Your enemy the devil prowls around like a roaring lion looking for someone to devour*" (**1 Peter 5:8**). It is interesting that the Greek word translated "*devour*" here is translated as "*drown*" in **Hebrews 11:29**. Basically, the enemy wants to drown our influence.

88

Some say they are Christians, but don't believe in a devil. I find that hard to understand because the Bible speaks of him. Jesus associated evil with Satan and his schemes. *"Ought not this woman, being a daughter of Abraham, whom Satan hath bound, lo these eighteen years, be loosed from this bond?"* (**Luke 13:16**). Many do not appear to take the devil seriously. They seemingly have the impression that when the Bible speaks of the devil, it is referring merely to an evil influence, an inordinate desire, or perhaps that natural tendency toward evil we all know is in our hearts. Nothing is further from the truth. The devil is a person. The Bible ascribes to him all the attributes of personality. The Model Prayer reminds us to fear the strategies or wiles of Satan.

Satan, as a personal figure and as an entity apart from Jesus Himself, tempted Him in the wilderness (**Matthew 4**). There was even a conversation between them. It has been said it was as though two rabbis were walking and talking together.

Spiritual warfare

It is a truly great day in a person's life when sin's fetters begin to loosen, when here and there a link of the chain weakens, and a bar in the prison breaks. When salvation comes, there is rejoicing in the presence of the angels of God (**Luke 15:10**). From that day on, however, there is someone who does not rejoice. Spiritual warfare begins and will continue as long as we are in the flesh. Paul describes the conflict in graphic terms when he declared that when he would do good evil was present with him. He pointed out that he did not do what he wished to do, but did what he did not want to do (**Romans 7:19-20**).

When we study the efforts of Satan, it is important that we understand spiritual warfare. As far as contemporary Christians are concerned, most are either ignorant or indifferent. So Satan continues to do his work as we cooperate with him unknowingly because we have not taken the time to equip ourselves.

Satan is not omniscient, omnipotent, or omnipresent. He is organized. There is an organized effort on the part of Satan to do his work in the world. In **Ephesians 5:12**, we are told that we do not wrestle against flesh and blood, but against principalities, powers, rulers, and spiritual hosts of wickedness. This is a presentation of the domain of Satan. His four-tiered hierarchy of organization is laid out clearly. The forces of evil are led by the commander-in-chief, Satan, who possesses a power beyond what we mortals know. It is clear in Scripture that he has under his command a great army of demons and fallen angels. His effort is

89

organized. There is a hierarchy in the domain of Satan.

Christians battle against the "wiles" of the devil (**Ephesians 5:11**). "Wiles" is a military term which means organized combat or plans of war or strategies or methodologies. Satan attacks lives and causes that defeat his plan. That is the reason all of us who are Christians feel so much of Satan's presence. He is not after those who belong to him. He is after those who want to defeat him. Christians are considered his enemies.

Satan hates the book of Revelation because it tells the final chapter in his life. It prophesies ultimate doom and the success of the One of whom he is so jealous, the Lord Jesus Christ. He doesn't want us to know the Truth.

Read the Bible carefully. It was Satan who led Lot into Sodom, drove Abram into Egypt, and influenced Peter to deny Christ. He caused Ananias and Sapphira to lie to the Holy Spirit. It was Satan who even dared to attack the Lord Jesus with temptations to entice Him to sin.

If he is not afraid to attack the Lord of glory, you and I should not be surprised to discover that he is not afraid to attack the most godly of God's people. He comes to the church today with divisions, to paralyze its ministry and scandalize its leaders.

We live in Satan's territory. This battle is not fought on neutral ground. It is not fought on God's ground, but in the enemy's territory. This is a war that is being waged in a foreign country for those of us who are Christians. The world, the flesh, and the devil are our common enemies and each knows how to maneuver us in order to entice us resulting in weakness and failure in our lives (**1 John 2:16**).

The Bible says the devil has as his purposes the blinding of sinners, the beguiling of Christians, and the buffeting or hurting or discouraging of those who belong to God. He will do anything he can to disturb the mind or deceive the heart or defeat the life. He is actively involved today with his presence in this world.

There are three primary focuses for Satan's attacks: the individual Christians, homes, and churches. He is after every individual Christian to destroy his life and influence. He is after every Christian home to destroy its unity, purity, and oneness. He is after the church of the Lord Jesus Christ to embarrass it publicly, to destroy it nationally, to erode its ministry, to discredit its leaders, and to wipe out its financial basis so it will no longer have a presence in this world of darkness. As he did in the early church in Jerusalem, he continues to work havoc wherever he can get a foothold (**Acts 8:3**).

There are several names given to the devil in the Scriptures.

The armor of God

It is possible to resist temptation. God has provided us with armor described in **Ephesians 6:10-18**. We have the Word of God and the Holy Spirit. We don't have to be defeated. Actually the devil does not have a place to stand in a Christian unless the Christian gives him the place (**Ephesians 4:27**). Through God's Word, the Holy Spirit can expose the most cleverly hidden minefield and uncover the most cunningly concealed snare the devil can concoct. While it is important not to *"be ignorant of Satan's devices"* (**2 Corinthians 7:11**), it is equally vital to understand the armor God has provided for His children.

Ephesians 6:10-18 is the warfare passage and must be fully understood and implemented in order for a believer to engage Satan as a prayer warrior. A full treatment is included in my book, **Spiritual Warfare**, which is based on twelve studies. It is available through our office.

The Bible tells us **we are in war**. We are not on a holiday. We are called to fight with unseen sources and the fight is real. "Wrestle" is a term of great intensity. It pictures a man with a grip on another man pressing hard, straining every muscle, to pin him to the ground. The child of God strains every moral muscle and tests every spiritual sinew. He uses every bit of energy to resist. Modern Christians have lost the sense of warfare and are easily defeated. They are walking around in the minefields with bullets flying over their heads totally unaware a war is going on and that they are considered by the adversary as the enemy.

Yet the Word of God tells us this warfare is one for which we can prepare. We don't have to go into battle unprotected. As we learn and apply the truths, we can walk out into a hostile environment and engage in warfare for God—and not be defeated. Our Commander-in-Chief has already won the war and He wants us to get in on the victory every day.

You can't win unless you are prepared. Take time to learn and understand the provisions God has made for our victory. The command is to "take unto you the whole armor of God." He did not tell us if we prayed right God would give us the armor. Neither does He instruct us to look around and see if we can find it and purchase it. Rather, it is the Christian's personal responsibility to appropriate the armor provided by God for his own life. It is not something God will do for us, but is something God commanded us to do for ourselves. Get the armor and put it on! It is our job to do that. Failing to put on the armor is disobedience which is sin and rebellion.

If you and I are defeated in the warfare—shot in an unprotected place—it is not God's fault. It is our duty to put it on. The armor will protect you from what the enemy wants to do to you.

Each piece of the armor specifically deals with some area of life which is the focus of Satanic strategy.

1. **The girdle of Truth.** The knowledge, the acceptance, and the use of Truth as it encircles your spiritual being is included in the girdle of Truth. It consists of the great truths of our God and His relationship to us through Christ. It includes a complete understanding of what God has said about Himself, His Son, and mankind. It is the knowledge of God which is resident in His Word. Bible doctrine is a better word. One ploy of Satan is to deceive people in Bible teaching churches who do not have a grasp on the Truth. Many join cults who take a little truth and uses it to deceive and mislead believers.

A believer is wise to take advantage of every opportunity to learn something about the Bible. This will help you be armed against the enemy who is after you.

A Christian's Necessary Food is the title of my book dealing with Bible study for a believer. Included are many practical suggestions to enhance your daily time in the Word. The book may be obtained through our office.

2. **The breastplate of righteousness.** This piece of equipment is desperately needed because this is the area where the darts are aimed. This equipment has two sides. The inside of the breastplate of righteousness is the righteousness of Christ which is absolutely impenetrable. The outside is our personal righteousness.

3. **The shoes of the gospel.** The shoes have to do with advancement of the cause of Christ through our witnessing. Obedience to witness is a part of our protection against the enemy. One never walks more closely to the Lord than when he is praying for courage to witness to those around him.

4. **The shield of faith.** The confidence in God's promises is an indication of our faith. Faith is simply believing God will do what He said He would do.

5. **The helmet of salvation.** The helmet obviously is to protect our minds. If a Christian is defeated, it will be in his mind. God is interested in our intellect and in the thinking process. We need protection from secular humanism and the immoral teachings characteristic of our day.

6. **The sword of the Spirit.** The only offensive weapon "which is the Word of God." Jesus used the Word when attacked by Satan when He took the sword and said "It is written." The ability of the Christian with the help of the Spirit to see life from God's point of view is basic—which is reflected by having a sharp sword to use. Many of our swords are dull because we do not know the Word and do not use it.

7. **The battle is prayer.** The first activity listed after the armor is on is prayer (**v. 18**). We will never win the war if we do not know where the battle is being fought.

God never sends us out to war without communication. He gives every Christian his own personal walkee-talkee so he can be in touch with His Commander-in-Chief as he walks in the world. No matter where the warfare is, we can pick up the walkee-talkee and use prayer as a weapon.

Victory is possible

When we learn to use the equipment God has given us, we can be victorious. We are not be to confident in our flesh. The command is to submit to God and resist the devil (**James 4:7**).

The Holy Spirit opens men's eyes to invisible enemies, too. Through the Holy Spirit, the Word of God shines like a light in the darkness. The Holy Spirit makes the Word of God a weapon of resistance, the shield that blunts the poison darks hurled by the evil one, the helmet of salvation, the breastplate of righteousness, and the sword of the Spirit. It is the armor we are asking for when we pray "*and lead us not into temptation, but deliver us from the evil one.*" He will answer our prayer. Christ will never let His own be tempted beyond their power of resistance.

When we pray, "*Deliver us from the evil one,*" we are recognizing and pleading for the greater power of God to work in our lives. God's faithfulness assures us that we will never be left alone as we live our lives in the enemy's territory. As we appropriate His provisions, victory will come on a daily basis.

Study Twelve

And when you pray, say, *"For Thine is the kingdom, and the power, and the glory forever. Amen."*

Matthew 6:13b

To appropriate God's provisions, a believer needs to understand prayer and its proper place in his life. The clear intention of the Lord Jesus Christ, when asked by one of the disciples to teach them to pray, was to provide information and insight to bring about that understanding.

Note that Jesus did not say that we are merely to repeat His prayer; rather, He said, *"After this manner, pray ye."* In other words, He set forth a model or pattern for His children to follow in their prayers. The Model Prayer, commonly termed The Lord's Prayer, is not so much a prayer to pray as it a prayer to teach us how to pray. Although I have long respected the Model Prayer, the intensive study which I have done leads me to conclude that any believer is wise to master the content as a foundation for his prayer life.

Prayer defined

There have been many efforts to define prayer clearly and concisely—and many ideas are shared during the six-hour prayer seminar—but the Greek word itself probably is as good a beginning point that one could have. The word is *proseuchee* made up of the preposition *pros* ("to") and *euchee* ("vow" or "wish"). *Euchee* comes from *eu* meaning "well" and the verb *cheoo*, "to pour out." Prayer then is a wish or a desire directed toward God.

One can illustrate the basic definition of prayer as a wish directed toward God by applying it to the Model Prayer: We wish that His name will be hallowed with proper reverence, for His Kingdom to come and His will to be done on earth as it is in Heaven. We wish for Him to supply our daily bread and our physical needs. We wish our sins to be forgiven. We wish not to be led and left alone in facing trials and temptations. We wish to be delivered from evil and the evil one.

Prayer encompasses adoration, confession, and thanksgiving. Certainly, a believer needs to include these three elements in daily praying. It is important to remember, however, that the word *pray* as used in **2 Chronicles 7:14** and **James 4:2b** is the word *ask* when we want God's hand to move either for ourselves (**petition praying**) or others (**intercessory praying**). The sovereign God has ordained prayer as the tool to get His work done. He works in concert with the praying of His children.

Further, the Scripture clearly teaches that both the Lord Jesus Christ and the Holy Spirit join us when we begin to pray (**Hebrews 7:25, Hebrews 9:24, 1 John 2:1, Romans 8:34,** and **Romans 8:26-27.** Both are identified by the Greek word *Paraclete* which means one called along side to help. In other words, both are our Helpers. Jesus pointed out, more specifically, that the Holy Spirit dwells **in** the believer (**John 14:17**) while Jesus Himself is on His throne in Heaven seated at the right hand of the Father making intercession for us. There could be no greater provision than what the Father has provided for us. Prayer is to the Father, through the Son, in the power of the Holy Spirit.

Review

During our in-depth studies on the Model Prayer, we have learned many basic principles. All prayer is to begin with praise—"*Our Father which art in Heaven, hallowed be Thy name.*" All prayer must reflect proper priorities—that "*Thy kingdom come, Thy will be done on earth as it is in Heaven.*" We have learned that it is right to come to God with our needs and ask for His provision: "*Give us this day our daily bread.*" It is proper to pray for wholesome personal relatonships and to those who are willing to forgive others even as they have been forgiven, that is indeed a possibility. We have learned that God is interested in our escaping the enemy and not walking through the mine-fields of his temptation. It is right to pray every day, "*And lead us not into testing, but in the midst of it deliver us from the evil one.*"

The last phrase—the doxology

The closing words of the Model Prayer are spoken of as "the doxology." The prayer begins with very impressive words of address, "*Our Father who art in heaven.*" The ending is equally impressive, "*For Thine is the kingdom, and the power, and the glory forever. Amen.*" As someone has said, "*The closing doxology is the blowing of all the trumpets.*" It is a precious ending to a precious prayer.

Prayer begins and ends with God. All prayer should begin with praise and end with praise. Praise is the bookends to hold prayer together. Between these two grand boundaries are seven petitions, the first three looking Godward and the last four looking manward. After worship, we are ready to take our needs to Him. Sadly, we are so prone to rush in with needs perceived so pressing that we fail to spend time in praise. When we do, our prayers lose their focus.

The first four thoughts in the Model Prayer are repeated in summary fashion in the last four words. The last phrase of the Model Prayer brings us back to where we began. It is a fitting ending. We are to pray "*Thy kingdom come.*" "*For Thine is the kingdom*" is the ending measure. There is the King in place ruling.

Then we pray "*Thy will be done*" and affirm with confidence, "*For Thine is the power.*" We ask that His name be "*hallowed*" and proclaim "*For Thine is the glory.*" We ask for provision and note that He is "forever."

This part of the Model Prayer is a New Testament echo of an Old Testament prayer that is seldom read since it is tucked away in **1 Chronicles 29:10-13**: "*Thine, O Lord, is the greatness, The power and the glory, The victory and the majesty; For all that is in heaven and in earth is Thine; Thine is the kingdom, O Lord, And You are exalted as head over all.*" David's prayer has as its focus the character of God. Clearly, it is the character of God that is highlighted in the doxology. When one places focus on who God is—His character, His attributes, His essence—his praying will be transformed. He will be able to get his eyes off self and on God. This is worship which is to come before we begin to bring our needs to God. This is the point which Jesus is making with His disciples.

Purpose of the doxology

What does the Model Prayer teach us about the character of God? There are four things in these last words. First, we must praise Him for His sovereignty—"*Thine is the kingdom.*" Second, we must praise Him for His authority—"*Thine is the power.*" Third, we are to praise Him for His majesty—"*Thine is the glory.*" Fourth, we praise Him for His eternity—"*forever.*"

The doxology keeps before us as we approach God in prayer the reasons why we feel confidence in approaching Him for the items included in the prayer. God's kingdom will never end; His power will never fail; and glory, credit, and praise should be His at all times and forever.

Our purpose is to give God His due, and encourage others to do likewise. From angels and mankind He is deserving of highest praise. In Heaven, He has it constantly. On earth many people do not praise Him, though called upon to do so. This doxology enables us actively to praise Him. We are to praise Him with our lips.

The kingdom

The doxology begins with an expression of belief in the sovereighty of God as King. The God whom we serve is the God whose kingdom is forever. The kingdom is glorious and will endure forever. His sovereignty, authority, integrity, and eternality are acknowledged. First of all, we must praise Him for His sovereignty, a word which means *final say*. Sovereignty means to be in control. The kingdom belongs to God who is the authority and sovereign over all.

We do well to emphasize the word *t h e*. God is acknowledged as not merely having a kingdom, but *the* kingdom, the supreme kingdom, the everlasting kingdom. Earth has had and still has its kings and its kingdoms, but there is one supreme King and kingdom. Earthly kingdoms rise and fall; His kingdom is forever.

The kingdom is the central theme of the Model Prayer. It is the only key word that occurs twice so we say "*Thine is the kingdom—the powerful kingdom—the glorious kingdom—the eternal kingdom.*" All powerful, glorious, forever. Amen!

One of the greatest evidences of His sovereignty is this. When God wanted a king, He choose His Son to be the King. He named Jesus Christ the King of the earth. His kingship is highlighted in the Scriptures. He is the King of heaven (**Daniel 4:37**), the King of the Jews (**Matthew 2:2**), the King of Israel (**John 1:49**), the King of the Ages (**1 Timothy 1:17**), the King of glory (**Psalm 24:7**), the King of the saints (**Revelation 15:3**), He is King of kings (**Revelation 19:6**), and He is the Prince of all the kings of all the earth (**Revelation 1:3**). He is King. Jesus Christ is the King. He is the sovereign Lord of the universe.

God is sovereign "in creation." Where did the world come from and how is it we inhabit it? The scientists debate the answer and even some theologians appear mixed up about it. But the Bible says "*He hath made the earth by His power. He has established the world by His wisdom, and He hath stretched out the heavens by His discretion*" (**Jeremiah 10:12**). God created the world. He is sovereign in creation.

Further, He is sovereign "over creation." "*When He uttereth His voice, there is a multitude of waters in the heavens and He causeth the vapors to ascend from the ends of the earth. He*

97

maketh lightenings with rain. He bringeth forth the wind out of His treasures" (**Jeremiah 10:13**). In graphic, personal language, Jeremiah said, "God speaks and it rains. He speaks and it thunders." He is not only the Creator of the universe, He is the Sustainer of the universe. He not only created it, but He keeps it going. God is in control.

God is not only sovereign in and over creation, He is sovereign in history. *"This decision is by the decree of the watchers and the sentence by the word of the holy ones, in order THAT THE LIVING MAY KNOW THAT THE MOST HIGH RULES in the kingdom of men, Gives it to whomever He will, and sets over it the lowest of men"* (**Daniel 4:17**). He is a hands-on God who is seen in the ebb and flow of history. In fact, history is HIS STORY. He has history in His hand. Further, He is sovereign *"in heaven"* (**Daniel 4:35**).

We are to *"Seek first the kingdom of God and His righteousness"* as our priority knowing that *"all these things shall be added unto you"* (**Matthew 6:33**). Whatever happens in our lives, we can know that God is in control.

The power

After we praise Him for His sovreignty, we praise God for His authority. He is not an absentee God who created the world by His sovereignty. He controls the world. He is active every day in energizing His kingdom. What He has created He controls. This doxology expresses belief in the infinite power of God. The verb is present, not future; *"is,"* not merely, *"will be."* In the prayer, we pray that God's Kingdom will truly come on earth. We pray that righteousness will prevail. We pray in confidence because all power now belongs to God and He is able by His power to bring to pass that for which we pray.

God's power is illustrated in many ways. He has established a covenant with His people and has always been faithful to it. He promised Abraham that through his seed all the earth would be blessed. Remember He gave Isaac to Abraham and Sarah when they were far past child-bearing years. Abraham trusted His promise even to the point of placing Isaac upon the altar of sacrifice because He believed God had the power to raise him up again (**Hebrews 11: 17-19**). Because of his confidence in the power of God, he went forth obediently.

God is omnipotent and we can trust Him to do what needs to be done. He has the power.

The glory

We praise God for His majesty. The doxology ends with *"And the glory"* which gives this part of the Model Glory Prayer its name "doxology." *Doxa* is the Greek word for "glory." Glory in the New Testament comes from a word which simply means *light*. Glory is light. *"God is Light and in Him there is no darkness at all"* (**1 John 1:5**). When glory is manifested in the Bible, you see light. Light is glory. In God is total light.

Glory calls for glorifying. Primarily this word means praise, adoring prayer to God. Whatever happens, God *is* glorious and is to be given glory. Praises belong always to God. He is to be honored, acclaimed, acknowledged for His love and justice, and praised from the heart. His holiness is such that He can do no wrong.

It is worth noting that the New Testament emphatically presents the glory of God in relation to the history of Jesus, and that in this connection the cross (as well as the resurrection) is of key significance The glory of God is seen as the glory of the Crucified, the glory of self-sacrificing love.

An element of delight, desire, and enjoyment is part of the response to God's glory. Our chief end is to glorify God and enjoy Him forever. Our focus even now is on His perfection and beauty. Once we glimpse who He is, we are transformed to walk with Him in obedience.

God is the glory of this world. The glory is there and we are reflectors of that glory to a lost world. The reason God is not more glorified in our world is because there are too many dirty reflectors. Light cannot reflect where dirt covers the reflecting surface. God wants to be the glory of this world. When we pray, *"Thine is the glory"* it means a great deal. It means that God is glorified. One day He will be ultimately glorified. Then it won't be necessary for God's glory to be dependent on feeble reflectors. What a great prospect we all have when God fills the earth with His own glory with no need for sun or moon. God Himself will be the brilliance of light.

Amen

Both the Old Testament and New Testament confess and extol the kingdom, the power, and the glory of the Lord. Thereby we express confidence knowing that the final hope of prayer does not rest on us—but on God's own faithfulness. As we pray, we do not look at our own good deeds or accomplishments, but at the God of promise Himself—at the

Mediator, the Lord Jesus Christ. Prayer is to be closed with an affirmation, "*so let it be.*" We can be assured that God hears and will bless our praying. Prayer is not a shout sent forth to someone in the distance who may, or may not, be interested in us. *Amen* confesses assurance of God's faithfulness—that He does hear and will respond as He sees fit.

The little word "*for*" leads to the proper conclusion of our praying. We pray because God is God with all sovereignty, all authority, and all majesty to certify His complete trustworthiness.

Conclusion

The Model Prayer is a letter sent from earth to Heaven. In the inscription of the letter is the name of the person to whom it is directed, "OUR FATHER"—the place where it is being sent, "WHICH ART IN HEAVEN"—the contents of it in the six requests: "HALLOWED BE THY NAME, THY KINGDOM COME, THY WILL BE DONE ON EARTH AS IT IS IN HEAVEN. GIVE US THIS DAY OUR DAILY BREAD, FORGIVE US OUR DEBTS AS WE FORGIVE OUR DEBTORS, AND LEAD US NOT INTO TEMPTATION, BUT DELIVER US FROM THE EVIL ONE"—the seal, "AMEN" and, if you will, the date, "THIS DAY."

The disciples became proficient in prayer as is attested by what was accomplished as they exemplified the work of the Master in Christian living and service when they literally turned their world upside down (**Acts 17:6**). We can be sure they followed the pattern Jesus taught in the Model Prayer in their own praying, and taught the pattern to new disciples. So should we.

John Wesley himself prayed the Model Prayer daily. A medieval practice was to repeat the Model Prayer in silence to prepare the soul for worship. Although a believer must caution against allowing the "repetition" to become a meaningless routine, praying the words themselves and meaning them in your heart, is an uplifting experience. Certainly we are wise to build our prayers around His pattern. Let's determine to implement His teaching in our own daily prayer times. It will make a difference and we will do well to do that very thing.

Prayer seminar helps you get started!

Most Christians know the important place of prayer in the life of a believer. I do not have to make a case with you about that.

But it is not easy to pray. It is easier to preach, to do youth work or the work of a deacon, to teach a Sunday school class, or to go visiting! Why is this?

I believe the reason Satan doesn't want a person to learn to pray is because prayer unleashes the power of God in the life of a believer. Satan trembles when he sees the weakest Christian on his knees. I will never win the war if I don't know where the battle is being fought. Prayer is the place!

What about your personal altar? Is it broken down and deserted? Take an inventory of your prayer life. What is happening in your life in answer to prayer? What about others in your church?

A prayer seminar could help you and other believers get started! Using the *Prayer Seminar Workbook* (79 pages), the six-hour prayer seminar teaches the importance of a proper and effective prayer life for the Christian and clearly demonstrates the spiritual impact every believer can generate through prayer. Over 700 seminars have been conducted in 43 states, the District of Columbia, Australia, the Bahamas, Costa Rica, England, Fiji Islands, India, Indonesia, Israel, Italy, Jamaica, Japan, Korea, Malaysia, Mexico, New Zealand, Nigeria, N. Ireland, Okinawa, the Philippines, Puerto Rico, Russia, Scotland, Singapore, Switzerland, Thailand, Ukraine, Venezuela, and Zambia.

HOW TO:
- Establish prayer as a daily priority.
- Organize your praying following a biblical pattern.
- Worship, praise, confess, and thank the Lord.
- Pray for yourself as well as others.

The prayer seminar is a faith ministry which trusts God to provide the financial needs through local churches and individuals. Therefore, we do not charge a set fee. Basically, participants are encouraged to contribute a one-time gift through the church love offering for the seminar as the Lord leads. Each participant receives a copy of the prayer seminar workbook, the basic teaching tool. A suggested contribution is $5 to defray the printing cost. Beyond the free-will offering, help with travel is necessary. If the Lord lays on your heart to host a seminar, however, do not hesitate to make contact with J. Gordon Henry Ministries about the travel expense, if that is a problem.

Seminars have been conducted with Baptist (various groups), Christian and Missionary Alliance, Church of the Brethren, Free Methodist, United Methodist, Presbyterian, Mennonite, Assembly of God, Conservative Congregational, Christian, Pentecostal, Evangelical Free, Lutheran, Pentecostal Free Will Baptists, Reformed, Christian Reformed, and independent Bible churches. In addition, there have been seminars in Bible colleges and liberal arts/colleges/universities. Prayer seminars have been conducted for state-wide men's retreats, summer camp meetings and/or retreats for special groups, such as pastors. Seminars have been conducted on military bases and in prisons.

For additional information about the seminar (including a sample copy of the workbook, letters of reference, and scheduling), write or call:

J. Gordon Henry Ministries
2114 Arrow Court
Murfreesboro, Tennessee 37127-5943
(615) 890-8384 (office)—M-F 8:00 A.M.-5:00 P.M. CDST
or
(615) 890-6264 (residence)